REFACING
CABINETS

REFACING CABINETS

MAKING AN OLD KITCHEN NEW

HERRICK KIMBALL

The Taunton Press

COVER PHOTO: **Susan Kahn**

for fellow enthusiasts

10 9 8 7 6 5 4 3 2 1

Printed in the United States of America

A Fine Homebuilding Book

Fine Homebuilding® is a trademark of The Taunton Press, Inc.,
registered in the U.S. Patent and Trademark Office.

The Taunton Press, Inc., 63 South Main Street, PO Box 5506,
Newtown, CT 06470-5506
e-mail: tp@taunton.com

Library of Congress Cataloging-in-Publication Data

Kimball, Herrick.
        Refacing cabinets : making an old kitchen new / Herrick Kimball.
            p.   cm.
        "A Fine homebuilding book"—T.p. verso.
        Includes index.
        ISBN 1-56158-197-6
        1. Kitchen cabinets—Remodeling. 2. Kitchen cabinets—Repairing.
    I. Title.
    TT197.5.K57K55   1997
    684.1'6—dc21   97-20244
                                                    CIP

To my work buddies in the legendary Ja-Well Construction crew from 1986-1988: Steve Bossard, Gerard Jones, Kenny Pearsall, Vance Vargason, and Steve Wellauer. Talented, driven, and slightly crazed—we were a rare bunch.

ACKNOWLEDGMENTS

Many special people played a part in putting this book together. My sincere thanks go out to the following:

Julie Trelstad, Fine Homebuilding books acquisitions editor, who, when I suggested the topic for this book, enthusiastically approved, and then shepherded the project through the appropriate channels.

Karen Liljedahl, Fine Homebuilding books assistant editor, who handles her many duties with grace and aplomb.

Ruth Dobsevage, my perspicacious editor, who does her job with such professionalism.

Susan Kahn, a most talented photographer. I feel fortunate that she took the photos for the book.

David Fuleihan, of Concepts in Wood, for his review of the manuscript and valuable comments.

Finally, special thanks to Tony and Patti Beaudry, Richard Clouthier, Bill and Pat Derenberger, Ron and Barb Estep, and Wayne and Marjorie Marks, who so graciously allowed us to photograph their kitchens.

CONTENTS

INTRODUCTION

Everything has a lifespan, and for the average kitchen it's around 20 years. There are, of course, exceptions to the rule, but in most instances, after a couple of decades that once gleaming new kitchen will be worn, outdated, and drab. While many components of an old kitchen can be upgraded with relative ease, the cabinetry is another story. Installing new cabinets is an involved proposition, and new cabinets are expensive. In fact, cabinetry is typically the most expensive component of a kitchen.

Although it is possible to improve the appearance of old cabinets by washing and waxing or sanding and refinishing, in most instances they won't look much better than what you started with. They certainly won't look anywhere near as good as new cabinets would.

If your kitchen cabinets are looking dowdy, don't despair. By making some simple changes to improve the efficiency of your existing cabinet layout and then refacing those cabinets, you can have a beautiful new kitchen for a fraction of the cost of ripping everything out and replacing it. What's

more, a cabinet refacing job is usually a lot less disruptive than a conventional cabinet replacement job.

Sometimes called cabinet front replacement or cabinet restyling, refacing is a process whereby older cabinets are renewed by removing the old doors and drawer fronts, resurfacing the cabinet face frames and sides, and then installing new doors and drawer fronts. There are several methods for refacing face frames but I use prefinished wood veneers (with wood door styles) and wrap them around the rails and stiles. The finished appearance is that of a new face frame. Several other modifications, like upgrading old drawers and slides or replacing a worn-out lazy Susan, can be done at the same time, too.

If done properly, reface kitchen remodeling will give you a new kitchen that can be expected to age gracefully for another 20 years or so before you have to update again. If you have some basic woodworking tools and skills, you can do your own cabinet refacing—it's surprisingly easy. Showing you how to save a lot of money and end up with a remarkably nice new kitchen by doing the work yourself is what this book is all about.

You should know that there are critics of refacing. In fact, I used to be one of them; I scoffed at the notion that refacing could be a legitimate remodeling option. But I don't feel that way any more, and I'd like to tell you why.

In 1988, with nine years of down-and-dirty kitchen remodeling under my belt, I took a position as the manager of a kitchen and bath store. It was during this stint in sales that I first heard of refacing. I knew nothing about the subject except that it involved putting new doors on old cabinets, and at the time the whole concept seemed rather crass and cheap to me. I reasoned that the only way a person could get a beautiful new kitchen of lasting quality was to rip out the old cabinets and put in new ones—preferably bought from me.

To make a long story short, I eventually quit the sales job and headed back to the field as a self-employed remodeling contractor. I took with me my bias against refacing, but it wasn't long before I had a change of heart. It came when I saw a well-crafted reface kitchen remodel and talked to the craftsman who did the work. I was amazed at the job he had done. I saw immediately that cabinet refacing could be a legitimate remodeling option, and a sensible one, too.

From my time in sales, I knew that while most homeowners sincerely want to buy top-quality cabinetry, they typically settle for lesser-quality cabinets that look good and are reasonably priced. That's because top-quality cabinets are surprisingly expensive. Cabinet manufacturers realize that outward appearances and price are the main factors the average buyer considers, so they wisely concentrate on putting the bulk of cabinet quality into the doors and frames. I've heard that as much as 80% of the expense of making a new cabinet is in the fronts. Indeed, on many brands of new cabinetry (even into the mid-price range) the only real evidence of quality is in the cabinet fronts.

That first kitchen reface I saw looked as good as any new cabinetry I had ever seen. Although the insides of the cabinets were not new, they were perfectly functional and made of better materials than some upscale cabinets. I concluded that over the years I had installed or sold many new kitchens to people who could have gotten a better-quality finished product for less money by refacing.

There was very little related to refacing that I hadn't already done as a cabinetmaker and kitchen remodeler, and what I didn't know I figured I could pick up easily enough, so I didn't waste any time lining up some reface jobs. And now here I am, six years later, with scores of reface kitchen remodels behind me, extolling the virtues of the craft. I'm just as excited, if not more so, about refacing today as I was the day I realized it could be much more than a hokey cover-up.

Cabinet refacing is done with the cabinetry in place in the kitchen, and the job is further simplified by having all the new doors custom made and finished to your specifications by a company that specializes in doing just that. Although you may certainly go to the trouble of making your own doors, you don't have to; most professional refacers and, for that matter, quite a few name-brand cabinet manufacturers have their doors made by a custom door maker. There is no reason you can't take advantage of those services as well.

Regardless of the style of your present kitchen, the newly refaced version can be virtually any style you want. A classic 1960s built-in kitchen of plain birch plywood doors can be transformed into an elegant cherry kitchen with traditional raised-panel doors. A kitchen with dark cabinetry—so common in the 1970s—can become light, clean, and stylish with natural maple or oak doors. Pick a wood, pick a door style, pick the look you want, and it can probably be done with refacing. It's even possible to take traditional face-frame cabinetry and reface it to end up with the simple lines of Euro-style frameless cabinetry with full-overlay doors. That's what I did when I refaced the cabinets in my own kitchen (see the sidebar on pp. 34-35).

As wonderful as I consider refacing, I'll be the first to admit that this approach to kitchen remodeling is not appropriate in every situation. In some instances, the existing cabinets are so poorly made that they don't provide a suitable foundation to reface over. I once looked at a prospective kitchen reface where the cabinet sides, face frames, and doors were made out of nailed-together ½-in. waferboard, and nothing was square or level. While it's typical to need to do some minor repair and cabinet rebuilding when refacing, that particular kitchen would have required a complete rebuild, and I recommended getting new cabinets. Manufactured "trailer" housing typically has chintzy cabinets, often with particleboard face frames, and they are not worth refacing either. But more often that not, older cabinets are well made and their carcases are constructed of plywood, which is arguably a much better material than the high-density particleboard so prevalent in today's new cabinetry. To be fair, I should state that particleboard for cabinet sides, bottoms, and shelves isn't necessarily a poor-quality construction material (and I've refaced over many particleboard cabinets). It's just not as good as plywood.

If your original kitchen is poorly designed and you are planning extensive changes in layout, refacing may not be the best solution. That isn't to say that you can't make some modifications to improve the layout, flow, and efficiency of your kitchen when refacing, because, as this book will show, you certainly can and should. But there is a point of diminishing returns, and, depending on the extent of the changes, refacing may not be practical.

Whether or not refacing will fit into your remodeling plans is a call you'll have to make on your own, but after reading this book you'll be better prepared to make an informed decision. If I were to hazard a guess, though, I'd say that reface remodeling can be a workable option in better than 75% of the kitchens out there.

This isn't to suggest that refacing, even when it's appropriate, is always a good value. It turns out there are different ways to reface cabinets, and some approaches are better than others. For example, I once refaced a kitchen that had been refaced five years earlier. The homeowner had paid a lot of money to have a refacing "professional" put wood-grain contact paper on the cabinet sides and face frames. The new doors were sections of particleboard covered with matching contact paper. I was told that the job looked decent for about a year, before the paper started peeling. The whole thing ended up looking worse than ever.

I consider cabinet refacing to be a skilled craft, and although it is not a difficult craft to learn and master, it should nevertheless be taken seriously. Fortunately there are many refacing craftsmen who take pride in their work, but there are also a few, like the contact-paper refacer, who look upon refacing as a way to make a quick buck. Unfortunately, it's the charlatans and the people who just don't know how to do a good job that give refacing a bad name.

This book is a guide to the reputable craft of reface kitchen remodeling. It is not an exhaustive treatment of the subject because that would be, well, exhausting for you to read, and confusing as well. What can be confusing is that there are so many different style combinations and several different ways to reface a cabinet. To make matters worse, refacing is a relatively new discipline and many refacers, like members of the craft guilds of medieval Europe, do not like to share their "secret" techniques. And there is no national cabinet refacing institute to declare and promote standards of excellence in the craft.

What you hold in your hands is essentially Herrick Kimball's methods for refacing cabinets. Though I do mention other methods of work, my focus is on my techniques, which have evolved from my first-hand experiences and my observations of other refacers' work, as well as information I've gleaned from various material suppliers.

My methods are not the only right way to reface kitchen cabinets, but they are sound and proven and will result in a nice finished product—one you can take great pride in. All my secrets are here. If you are new to refacing, use this book as a primer to guide you through a reface job for yourself or launch you on a career as a reface professional. If you already are a professional, you'll still be able to pick up some helpful insights into the craft.

Chapter 1 covers the fundamental and essential topic of cabinet style, so you can decide how you want your new kitchen to look. Chapter 2 deals with the practical aspects of design by looking at several ideas for improving the organizational efficiency of your existing kitchen. Chapter 3 covers the tricky topic of measuring your kitchen for new doors and drawer fronts, and Chapter 4 takes a close look at the materials used for refacing and explains how to order them. In Chapter 5 we roll up our sleeves and get to work by prepping the old cabinets and resurfacing the sides and face frames. Chapter 6 explains how to veneer the face frames; Chapter 7 covers refacing with plastic laminate. And Chapter 8 describes hanging the doors, as well as installing drawers, valances, molding, and everything else you need to do to finish the job. The book concludes with a resource list, some suggestions for obtaining further information, a glossary, and an index.

Compared to many skills within the building trades, cabinet refacing is relatively safe, but it's not entirely benign. If you undertake any of the tasks outlined in this book, you must take responsibility for your own safety by educating yourself about the proper use of all power and hand tools, and observing all prudent safety precautions.

Finally, I welcome your feedback about this topic of refacing. In particular, I'm interested in hearing about any unusual experiences, solutions to problems, special techniques, and product insights. Please direct your comments to me c/o Fine Homebuilding Books, The Taunton Press, 63 South Main St., Newtown, CT 06470. If you include a self-addressed stamped envelope, I will reply by passing along any new tips or valuable information that come my way.

AN OVERVIEW OF REFACING

Since cabinet refacing is a relatively new craft, some readers may have only a vague idea of what refacing entails. Therefore, to put the subject in perspective, I want to give you a visual overview of the refacing process here, at the start, focusing on refacing with wood and wood doors.

1. The existing doors and drawer fronts are removed and discarded. They will be replaced with new custom-made and sized doors and drawer fronts.

2. Cabinet sides are typically sheathed with ¼-in. hardwood plywood that has been prefinished to match the new doors that will be installed. The same material may be used to cover the cabinet bottoms.

3. After the face frames are properly prepped, a flexible wood veneer is applied and wrapped around the front and edges of the face-frame rails and stiles.

4. New doors and hinges are installed, and new opening hardware is put on. Refaced kitchens can be restyled using virtually any door style available.

1

CABINET STYLE

Good kitchen design has two components: aesthetics (how the kitchen looks) and function (how well it works). The best designs take into account everything from lighting to color coordination. In this book, however, our concern is design as it relates to the refacing of cabinets. We'll begin by addressing the aesthetic issues related to cabinet style. You first need to decide how you want your new kitchen to look when it's done; the refacing materials and techniques you'll use to do the job will depend on the choices you make.

If you're like most people, you know exactly what you like and don't like when you look at different styles. So rather than offer you style guidelines here, I'll discuss the components of cabinet refacing style, which include doors, drawer fronts, pulls, hinges, valances, soffits, and moldings. Also included are pertinent insights and a bit of personal opinion. All of this should help you decide on a style that best suits your sensibilities and tastes. For additional ideas, and examples of how certain woods, doors, and colors can look in a finished kitchen, I highly recommend that you visit kitchen showrooms, collect cabinet sales literature, and search through the many

different home magazines on the market. Remember, almost anything that can be done with new cabinetry can be done with refacing.

DOORS

The single most important style decision you have to make is what kind of cabinet doors to use, and there are many choices to consider. First is the matter of what the doors will be made of: wood, plastic laminate, or vinyl. Then there is the matter of color. Last, but certainly not least, is the door design: slab, flat panel, raised panel, and so on.

To my mind, nothing can match the natural beauty and charm of real wood, and in most of the kitchens I've refaced, the homeowners have opted for wood doors. However, wood does have a few drawbacks. For one thing, it is an imperfect material; by that I mean it has unpredictable grain patterns, knots, mineral streaks, and color variations. Most people find the natural irregularities to be pleasing, but some consider them blemishes. Wood doors also require some special considerations in the area of care and maintenance. Though modern surface finishes are considerably more durable than those in years past, they are still

This old kitchen (left) was 26 years old and had built-in plywood cabinets. For its age, it wasn't in bad shape, but it dated the house. The home-owner wanted a new look. (Photo by Herrick Kimball.)

In the refaced kitchen (below), the old cabinets are still there underneath the new faces.

This kitchen once had traditional-style wood doors similar to the old kitchen shown in the top photo on p. 7. The cabinetry was refaced using full-overlay laminate doors with hidden cup-style hinges.

somewhat fragile; you can't scrub dried food spills off with abrasive cleaning agents (warm water and soap please, and no waxing should be needed). Also, wood can only take so much abuse (e.g., from an energetic two-year-old beating on the doors with a toy) before they scratch, dent, or, worse yet, chip and splinter.

In contrast, plastic-laminate doors are uniform in color. Even if you opt for a laminate with an imitation wood-grain pattern, the grain will be "naturally" perfect. Food spills on laminate clean off very easily (mild abrasive cleansers are usually acceptable, except with gloss finishes), and for the most part, laminate is more resistant to minor impact damage than wood.

When you compare laminate to wood, laminate seems to have the practical advantage, but when you're considering overall style, aesthetic considerations typically carry more weight. When people see a newly refaced kitchen with laminate doors, they'll say, "Yes, this is very nice." But when people see a kitchen refaced with doors that are made of wood, they'll say, "Wow, this is beautiful!"

Long term, wood doors have a distinct edge over laminate doors. If someday a door has to be replaced or if you want to install new cabinets with doors that match the old, it should be relatively easy. But with plastic laminate, colors fade and patterns are discontinued, so matching new doors with the old might be difficult, if not impossible.

Wood

To date, every kitchen that I've refaced with wood doors has had doors of the hardwoods oak, cherry, or maple. From a national perspective, oak has been virtually the standard-issue wood choice with new kitchens for many years, and it still remains the number-one seller, but in recent years, cherry and maple have been closing the gap. Other native hardwoods such as ash, birch, walnut, and hickory are also available from reface-door suppliers, and you may want to use them to get the look you want. Pine, a softwood, is another possibility. In this book, however, our discussion of woods will focus on oak, cherry, and maple.

Species Oak is available in red or white, which is a distinction between species as well as color. Of the two, red oak is by far the more commonly used wood because of the distinct look imparted by its naturally reddish-orange tone (see the photo at top right). Northern-grown red oak is widely regarded as superior to southern-grown varieties because the grain is much clearer. Oak is open grained (relatively porous), and this does not allow for a perfectly smooth surface finish. It finishes well enough, but if viewed closely or felt with the fingertips, the surface is somewhat rough and pitted. This isn't by any means a bad thing—it's just a characteristic of the wood. Another characteristic is the distinct contrast between the light and dark color tones in the grain (these are more obvious on dark-stained oak). Appearance aside, oak is very dense. If banged into, oak usually shows less damage because of its surface roughness and the variations in grain color. Oak has what I would describe as a "country" look about it.

Red oak is an open-grained wood and the most popular choice for wood cabinet doors and face frames. It is hard and durable. A clear finish (board at far left) brings out the attractive natural orange tones of the species.

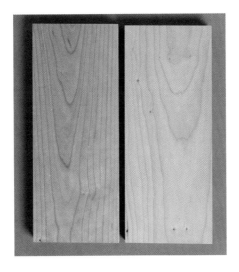

Cherry is a close-grained wood that finishes smoother than oak (board at far left is clear finished), though it is not quite as hard or durable. Cherry's natural color develops a dark red-brown patina over time (neither of these samples is aged).

In many respects, cherry (black cherry, a forest timber, not the orchard tree), is the opposite of oak. Cherry (see the photo above) is a close-grained wood, which allows for a very smooth finish, and cherry's grain pattern, though attractive and distinctive, is more subtle than oak's. One of the most favored properties of cherry is that its pinkish color mellows with age and develops a rich reddish-brown patina. While all woods darken a bit with age and exposure to sunlight, none does so as gracefully as cherry. However, cherry sapwood is white and does not darken like the heartwood. Because of

Hard maple (board at left is clear finished) has a grain that is in many ways similar to cherry, but it does not have the red tones of cherry and is a somewhat harder wood. Hard maple is the lightest-colored domestic wood.

this, the sapwood is not desirable on the face of doors. It's also typical for cherry to have dark pitch streaks and pockets scattered throughout. To my mind, cherry is a more upscale wood than oak; with a clear finish it has a simple, classy look about it. With darker stains, it has an elegant richness.

Maple is a close-grained wood, and it's available in a soft or hard species. Hard maple is marginally harder than soft maple, and it's also lighter colored (see the photo above). In fact, hard maple is the whitest of all domestic hardwoods (with the sapwood being the absolute whitest). Because maple has a grain similar to cherry but costs slightly less than cherry, it is often given a cherry stain and substituted for the real thing. That's why the wood is often referred to as "poor man's cherry." A not so desirable characteristic of maple is that it has dark-brown to black knots and streaks, which should be kept to a minimum on the door faces. I've refaced a couple of kitchens using maple doors with a clear finish, and the effect is a clean, natural, bright look that you can't get from any other wood.

Eastern white pine, a softwood, is much less durable than oak, cherry, or maple. Nevertheless, pine is sometimes used for cabinet doors. In fact, the wood is well suited to making primitive Early American style doors that will be painted and distressed to simulate age. Otherwise, I don't recommend pine for cabinet doors.

Color The finished color of wood doors depends on whether they're given a clear finish, stained, or painted. Clear finishes protect the wood without obscuring any of the natural "imperfections," such as tonal color differences between glued-together boards, unpredictable grain patterns, sap streaks, or knots. Because these variations become obvious—even highlighted—with clear-finished doors, many refacers have a disclaimer form they require their customers to sign before they'll reface with a naturally finished door. The essence of the form is that it's the nature of wood to be imperfect, clear finishes make the imperfections clearly visible, and you agree to be happy with whatever you get in this regard. A good door manufacturer will make a conscious effort to match up wood pieces for best effect on the front of the door (major blemishes go on the back side). And many door makers have a separate (higher) price level for using Select grades of wood. Still, you never know for sure exactly how the grain of a clear-finished door will look.

A little stain color will go a long way toward evening out minor tone variations, and a lot of stain color will go even further. However, with dark stains, the natural grain is substantially obscured (and dark colors may be a bad choice in poorly lit or small kitchens). Door manufacturers typically offer a range of stock stain colors for you to choose from. Sample stain blocks (see the photo at right) are usually available for a fee. Some manufacturers will even go to the trouble of custom color matching if you require it.

Closely related to stains are what I call washes (see the photo below). Typically white, these finishes are stains that are sprayed on a door before it gets a final clear finish. A thin wash gives a bleached, or "pickled," look to the door and allows more wood grain to show through than a heavier wash would. Washes are typically used on light-colored woods like maple, but washed doors of oak are also an option. Washes look nice, but they can present problems. Washes have been known to fade (allowing the grain to become more dominant) or yellow with age. Another shortcoming of light-colored washes is that on frame-and-panel doors, a hairline crack may develop in the finish at the joints where the frame pieces meet. This is a result of opposing dimensional move-ment in the pieces, and it's an aesthetic problem, not a structural

These rows of sample stain blocks show oak (top), cherry (middle), and maple (bottom) with a clear finish (left) and a light, medium, and dark stain. These are just a few of the possible stain colors that can be used.

Whitewashed maple. Washes are thinned stains. A light wash (left) will show more of the natural grain of the wood than a heavy wash (right).

Slab doors are usually installed as full-overlay doors with hidden cup hinges. This oak slab door and drawer front are made of oak veneer applied over a core of medium-density fiberboard.

door is a thing of beauty, it won't stay that way for long when exposed to the everyday wear that most kitchen doors receive. There is also the matter of getting an equally fine spray-painted finish on the existing cabinet face frames and sides (veneer would not be appropriate). Because spray painting requires specialized equipment and a certain amount of skill, I don't cover it in this book.

If you really want the light-colored look of a washed or painted door without the disadvantages, you might consider clear-finished hard maple, plastic laminate, or rigid thermal foil (RTF) doors. (Rigid thermal foil, a moldable type of vinyl plastic, is discussed on pp. 24-25.) If these alternatives are not to your liking, then go with the washed style. And a kitchen with light washed doors does look very nice.

Style Species and color aside, wood doors are available in a vast array of styles but the selection can be simplified by grouping the choices into one of four different types of doors: slab, plank, frame and flat panel, and frame and raised panel.

one. Because of these problems, many refacers require a customer to sign a release form for washed finishes, just as with the clear finishes.

From an installer's point of view, prefinished veneers with a wash may or may not be able to be wrapped around face frames like stained veneers, because the stain has been known to crack or flake off when the veneer is bent. If that happens, the damage isn't easily repaired. To get around this problem, the veneer must be applied to the faces only, and the inside edges of the frames are painted by hand to match.

Painted doors are another color option, but they have all the same problems as washed doors, and then some. Although a finely spray-painted

Slab doors (see the photo above left) are the simplest type of door, and as their name indicates, they are nothing more than a flat piece of wood. Slabs are made of plywood (⅝ in to ¾ in. thick) with good face veneers, or, more typically, of medium-density fiberboard (MDF) with veneer applied to both sides. Of the two, MDF is probably the better choice because it has more dimensional stability than plywood and is therefore less likely to warp. In either case, the edges of the door are usually covered with matching strips of veneer.

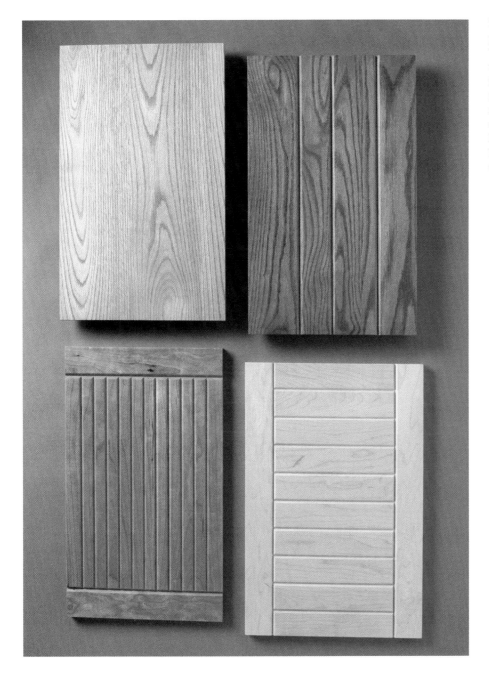

Plank doors can be flat and plain (top left) or grooved. These doors, clockwise from top left, are oak with a clear finish, oak with a "nutmeg" finish, maple with a clear finish, and cherry with a clear finish. The oak doors have horizontal batten boards on their back sides to help prevent warping.

As you might guess, slab doors are the least expensive wood-door choice, but that doesn't mean they can't look very nice. I think they look best when installed as full-overlay doors (see the sidebar on pp. 22-23). The smooth and flat surface of slab doors allows them to be wiped clean with relative ease.

Plank doors (see the photo above) are made of solid wood boards glued together to form a panel. You'll note in the photo that the oak plank door at top left looks somewhat like the oak slab door in the photo on the facing page, except for the appearance of the grain. That's because the slab door is

Flat-panel doors have a solid wood frame and a flat plywood or solid-wood panel. From left, a cathedral style in cherry with "harvest gold" stain, a "square" panel oak with "harvest gold" stain, and clear-finished maple.

FRAME-AND-PANEL DOOR

Panel

Rail

Stiles

Rail

With a frame-and-panel door, solid-wood rails and stiles make up the frame that surrounds a center panel.

veneered and the plank door is solid wood, and veneers are cut out of a log differently than boards are.

Since solid wood has more dimensional instability than plywood or MDF, plank doors often have battens attached to their backs, or breadboard end pieces to help prevent warping. A more realistic plank look is sometimes achieved by cutting grooves in the face of the panel (and this also helps to relieve warp-causing stresses). The overall effect is somewhat rustic.

Frame-and-panel doors consist of a solid-wood frame that surrounds a panel (see the drawings at left and on the facing page). The horizontal top and bottom pieces of the frame are called the rails, and the vertical side pieces are the stiles. Flat-panel doors (see the photo above) usually have a thin (1/4-in.) center panel of solid wood or plywood. Raised-panel doors (see the photo on the facing page) have a thicker (1/2-in. to 3/4-in.) center panel. So that the panel can fit into the narrow grooves of the door frame, the edges must be shaped down to reduce their thickness, and this molded profile gives the panel a distinctive raised look.

Raised-panel doors have a solid-wood frame and a solid-wood center panel. These three doors are oak (left), cherry (middle), and maple (right). All three are stained with the same "colonial cherry" stain.

RAISED AND FLAT PANEL TYPES

With frame-and-panel doors, the panel fits into a groove milled into the rails and stiles.

Frame and solid wood—raised

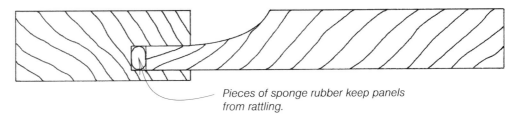

Pieces of sponge rubber keep panels from rattling.

Frame and solid wood—flat

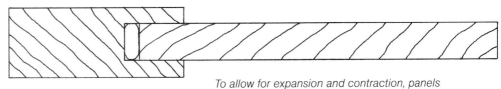

To allow for expansion and contraction, panels of solid wood are not glued in; they float freely.

Frame and ¼-in. plywood

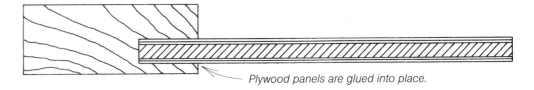

Plywood panels are glued into place.

Door frames may have butted mortise-and-tenon construction (left) or mitered construction (right). Mitered doors are more expensive and less common. These doors are both clear-finished cherry.

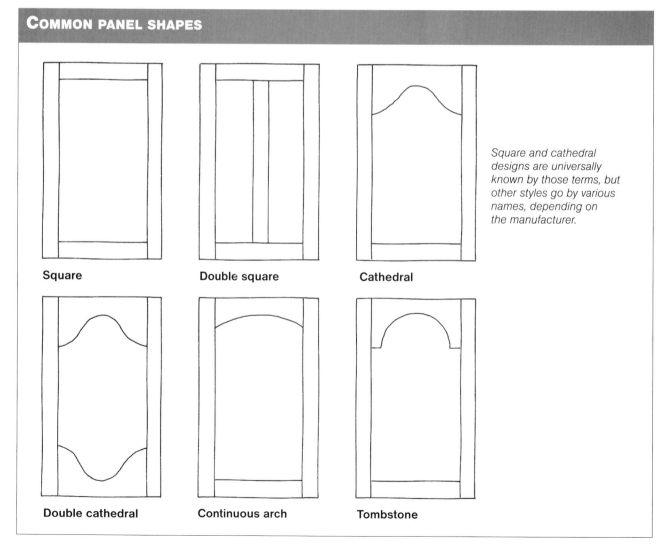

COMMON PANEL SHAPES

Square

Double square

Cathedral

Square and cathedral designs are universally known by those terms, but other styles go by various names, depending on the manufacturer.

Double cathedral

Continuous arch

Tombstone

Frame profiles

Panel profiles

Outside   Inside

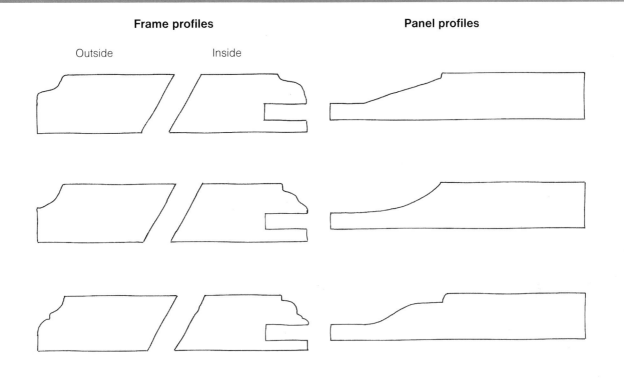

You can mix and match panel profiles with molded details on the outside and inside of the frame to get different styles. Just these 9 profiles can be combined to create 27 different door designs.

A further distinction with frame-and-panel doors is the type of construction method used to join the rails and stiles. As you can see in the photo on the facing page, a butted mortise-and-tenon joint is most common, but mitered corners are another possibility, and they do make a difference in overall appearance. Mitered door frames are used only on square panel doors (please note that the term "square panel" includes, and usually means, rectangular shapes).

With both flat-panel and raised-panel doors, the center panel can assume various shapes (see the drawing on the facing page). A cathedral shape is the most common design, and when cathedral doors (or any other type of arched profile doors) are used in a kitchen, they are generally placed on the upper cabinets. Square panels go on the bottom cabinets.

With a raised-panel door, the shaped profile of the panel can vary (see the drawing above). Door manufacturers typically offer several choices. To complicate matters even more, a panel profile is not the only profile you'll need to decide on. You'll also have to choose a detail on the outside and inside of the door frame. Here again, door makers usually offer a variety of choices. For example, the three raised-

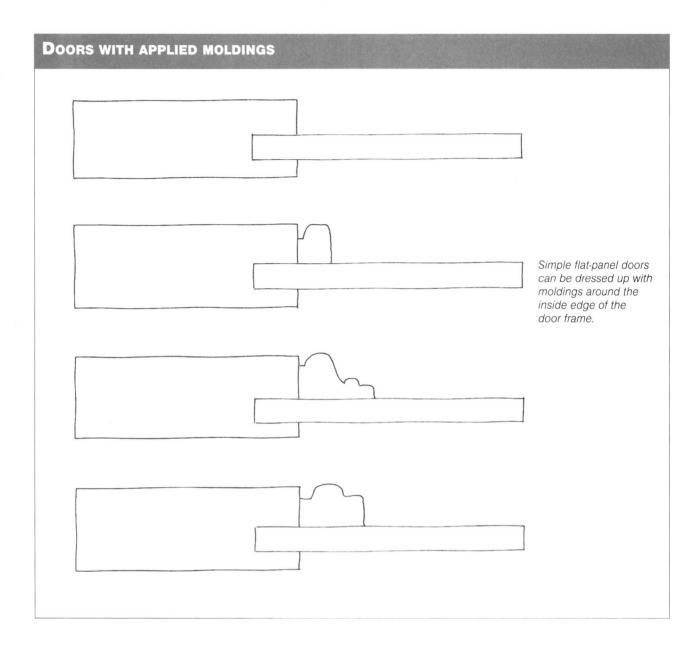

Simple flat-panel doors can be dressed up with moldings around the inside edge of the door frame.

panel doors in the photo on p. 15 each have different profile options on the panel raises and edges. Flat-panel doors can also have a detail cut along the inside and outside of the frame pieces. Alternatively, separate pieces of molding are sometimes applied around the inside edge (see the drawing above).

If you find all these options to be a bit mind-boggling, here's how you can substantially simplify your profile deci-

sion process. Find a picture of a door you like in a magazine or product literature, and then ask your door maker to match it as closely as possible with his particular selection of profiles. Another approach is to select a profile from the door manufacturer's sales literature. First, disregard any profiles you definitely don't like, and then narrow the remaining profiles down to one using the eeny-meeny-miney-mo approach. I'm not being flippant—

the point is that, unless you have a clear preference, selecting a profile needn't be a big deal because many of the choices are very similar, and the aesthetic differences are minor.

It's also possible to get doors without any center panel (these are called frame-only doors), with frames that are rabbeted out around the inside edge to allow you to install a pane of clear or leaded glass from the back.

Stained-glass panels, or clear and colored glass with custom etched designs, are some different glass possibilities. A further option is to add wood mullions (in the world of millwork, mullions are also known as muntins) to give the glass a divided-lite appearance (see the photo above). The mullions have a flat back side that the glass fits against, so one large piece of glass is all that's needed. Authentic divided lites (separate panes of glass) are also available.

The individual glass openings in mullion doors are called lites. Almost any arrangement of lites is possible.

Mullion doors are typically made so that one piece of glass, fit in from the back, serves as glazing for all the lites in a door.

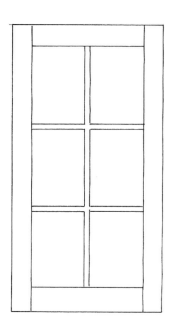
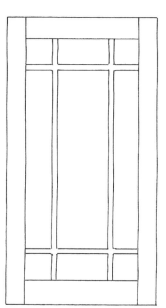
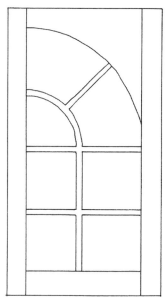

Different mullion configurations can really make an impact on kitchen style (see the drawing above).

However, if you are considering using mullioned doors with clear-glass inserts, keep in mind that the interior of the old cabinets will be visible. Depending on their condition, this may not be acceptable—dark or opaque glass may be called for.

Plastic laminate

Plastic-laminate doors are a European import that flourished in this country during the 1980s, and they still remain popular. When laminate cabinet doors are used, it's almost always with a Euro-style look, which is characterized by full-overlay doors (see the sidebar on pp. 22-23). The "classic" Euro-kitchen features white or almond-colored slab doors. The overall effect is clean, bright, streamlined, and aseptic—the style is particularly suited to hospitals and commercial offices. As for residential kitchens, I've found that most people—at least in upstate New York, where I live and work—aren't keen on the idea of laminate doors. Less than 10% of the kitchens I've refaced have been laminate styles. Nevertheless, laminate doors do have a practical, appealing quality, and I'm sure they'll be around in one form or another for as long as wood.

Laminate door slabs (see the photos on the facing page) are generally constructed of $5/8$-in.-thick MDF with vertical-grade plastic laminate applied to the fronts and backs. The resulting door thickness is just under $3/4$ in. White and almond-colored laminate remain the most popular colors, but they are by no means the only ones

Plastic-laminate doors and drawer fronts come in various styles. White laminate with a continuous wood pull (top right) is the typical Euro-style design, but some people prefer the look of an artificial wood-grain pattern (bottom right).

The term "overlay" refers to the location of the door relative to its frame. The type of door overlay you select will make a big difference in how your refaced kitchen will look, and it will also affect the door sizes you'll need to order as well as the type of hinges you'll need to hang the doors. Doors can be hung with a traditional-overlay style, or a more modern full overlay (see the drawing below. Or they can be inset, which means they have no overlay, or partially inset.

With a traditional overlay, relatively wide bands of cabinet face frame show between and around the doors. With a full-overlay style, the bands around the doors are comparatively small, just enough to allow the doors to open freely. Traditional overlays are used with traditional cabinets, which have a face frame. Full overlays are used with Euro-style cabinets, which do not have a face frame; the cabinet doors close against $3/4$-in.-wide cabinet sides.

When refacing, it's entirely possible for full-overlay doors to be hung on traditional cabinets, but traditional overlays can't be used on Euro-style cabinetry unless you first apply a face frame. Plastic-laminate doors usually look best when hung with a full overlay, but they don't have a monopoly on the style; virtually any kind of wood door can also be a full overlay.

Full-overlay doors will need to be hung using a cup hinge, which is hidden behind the door (see pp. 81-84 for more information on cup hinges). Traditional-overlay doors can also be hung using cup hinges, but such doors typically have traditional cabinet hinges that mount to the face frames and are partially visible on the front of the cabinets (see the photo on p. 28). You can see the overall difference in appearance between the two overlay styles in the before and after photos of my kitchen in the sidebar on pp. 34-35. The kitchen before refacing had doors with a traditional overlay and visible hinges, and the refaced kitchen has full-overlay doors with no visible hinges.

It's important to note that using cup hinges and a full-overlay style when refacing over face-frame cabinetry will not actually give you a true full overlay; the spacing between the doors will be around $1/2$ in. With frameless cabinetry and the proper cup hinges, full-overlay doors can be hung with about $1/8$ in. (or less) spacing all around. For most people, the distinction between a refacing full overlay and a true full overlay is not substantial enough to worry about,

Traditional and Euro-style cabinets

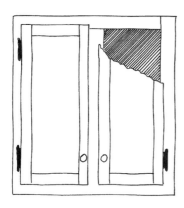

Traditional face-frame cabinet with traditional-overlay doors

Doors are hung with traditional hinges or cup hinges made specifically for face-frame applications.

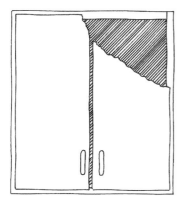

Euro-style frameless cabinet with full-overlay doors

Doors are hung using cup hinges only.

Variable- and fixed-overlay hinges

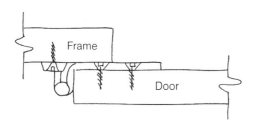

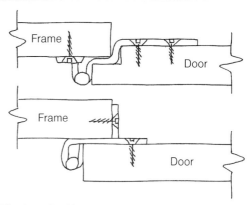

The variable-overlay hinge is the standard type of hinge used when refacing with traditional-style hinges.

Fixed-overlay hinges, including those on partially inset doors (top) are configured such that little, if any, side-to-side adjustment is possible.

but there is, nonetheless, a difference. If your existing kitchen has traditional-overlay doors, they have either a fixed- or a variable-overlay hinge (see the drawing above). On many older cabinets, the fixed-overlay hinges are on partially inset doors.

When refacing, the usual approach is to change fixed-overlay doors and hinges to a variable-overlay style. With the latter, you have much more latitude in sizing doors and adjusting face-frame reveals to achieve a more consistent and harmonious spacing (see pp. 55-59). Another reface possibility is to have inset doors (see the drawing at right). However, since inset doors fit in an opening instead of over it, refacing with inset doors would most likely require that the existing cabinet face frames be completely removed (assuming that you're working with traditional face-frame cabinets) and replaced with new face frames. This would be necessary because most existing face-frame

rails and stiles would be unnecessarily wide (and not look right), and the door openings probably wouldn't be precisely square (an absolute necessity). It is considerably more difficult to reface with inset doors than with overlay doors.

I haven't yet refaced a kitchen using an inset-door style, and would probably try to talk a customer out of it because of the extra fuss and

expense. If I were to do an inset job, I would forego the veneer and shop-build my face frames out of solid wood. They would be sized to accommodate all the cabinet openings in each straight run of cabinets. After knocking off the old face frames, I would attach the new ones with countersunk screws in pocket holes and glue blocks from the back side. I know one refacer who goes this route quite often.

Inset doors

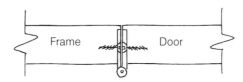

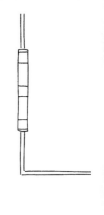

Inset doors are hinged with a butt-style hinge and fit into the face-frame openings, instead of over them; there is no overlay.

Rigid-thermal-foil (RTF) doors are made by forming a sheet of vinyl over a decorative door blank of MDF. Various colors are available.

available. Literally hundreds of colors, patterns (including woodgrains), and textures can be used.

Plastic-laminate door edges can be banded with the same plastic laminate used on the faces (referred to as self edge), but this is seldom done because the laminate has a dark phenolic back that shows as a black line at the edges (especially on light-colored doors). It's more common to band the edges with a strip of matching PVC plastic.

Another edge option is to apply solid wood strips (oak is typical) around the perimeter of each door. And yet another possibility is to band the sides with PVC and then attach a length of solid wood with an integral finger pull molded into it. In the trade this pull is called a continuous wood pull (CWP).

Rigid thermal foil (RTF)

Close cousins to laminate doors are thermo-formed vinyl doors (see the photo above). The vinyl, also called rigid thermal foil (RTF), is essentially a sheet of plastic that is heated up and vacuum pressed over the front and sides of ¾-in. MDF door shapes. An adhesive is sprayed on the MDF prior to forming. RTF door styles range from basic slabs to a variety of raised-panel profiles that have been milled into the face of the MDF using expensive CNC (computer numeric control) routers. The back of the doors have a melamine layer that is bonded to the MDF sheets before they're cut up into door sizes.

RTF raised-panel door styles in white resemble raised-panel doors with a painted finish, but they do not have the sharpness of detail at inside corners (they're rounded to some degree).

The vinyl is considerably more durable than paint, and because the front surface is one molded sheet of plastic, it's easy to keep clean. However, unlike plastic laminate (which can withstand solvents like acetone and mineral spirits and can usually be cleaned on occasion with gentle abrasive cleansers), RTF doors must be cleaned with soap- or alcohol-based cleaning agents. Abrasive cleansers, even mild ones, should never be used.

RTF doors are not recommended for use in humid places like saunas and greenhouses because the excessive moisture in such areas will cause swelling and delamination of the vinyl layer. (To be fair, it should be noted that extreme moisture conditions can cause problems with any door made of wood or wood byproducts.) In addition, direct sunlight may cause premature yellowing of white doors. I say premature yellowing because a color change over time with any kind of white door is inevitable. Whether or not the vinyl will discolor faster or more readily than plastic laminate, I can't say for certain. I do know that I installed a new kitchen with white RTF doors six years ago (not in direct sun) and it still looks white to me, so I don't think yellowing is necessarily a problem with vinyl doors.

Besides white, there are other RTF color and pattern options, including some wood grains, but the selection isn't nearly as extensive as with plastic laminate. Also, if an RTF door needs to be replaced years (or maybe even a year) later, there is no guarantee that the manufacturer will still be in business, or that the color and pattern of the door will still be in stock. Mullioned vinyl doors and a limited selection of vinyl moldings are also available.

Wood drawer fronts can be simple flat planks or have a profile milled into the edges. These three are oak with a clear finish. The middle one is made with 4/4 lumber while the one on the bottom is of 5/4 lumber.

DRAWER FRONTS

Drawer fronts should conform to the style of door you use (see the photo above). Slab fronts naturally go with slab doors; flat solid-wood plank fronts are appropriate for plank and simple flat-panel door styles. (To maintain continuity of terminology in this book, I will use the term "plank" when referring to fronts made of solid wood. However, you should be aware that many door makers use the term "slab.") Some door suppliers also offer frame-and-panel drawer fronts that are, essentially, mini-doors applied horizontally, though they are available only in square (rectangular) panels. There's no such thing as a cathedral-style drawer front.

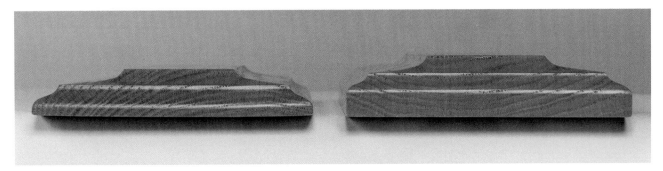

The extra thickness of a 5/4 drawer front (above right) lends a more substantial look, and it also provides more wood to fasten into when the front is attached to the drawer and screws are driven into the back side. The drawer front on the left is 4/4.

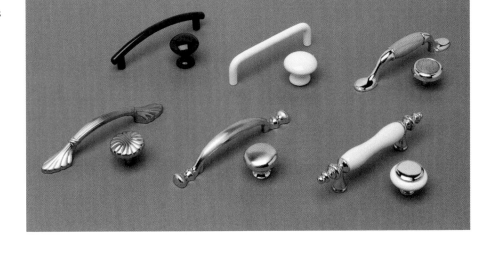

These knobs and pulls represent just a few of the thousands of available hardware options.

I've never used frame-and-panel drawer fronts because my door supplier doesn't offer them, and they're relatively expensive anyway. When I want a decorative front to go with something like a raised-panel door, I get planks with a raised profile on the edges, and I think they look just fine. When ordering raised planks, I always specify that they be made from 5/4 stock, as opposed to the regular 4/4 stock. (The fractional designations indicate the thickness of roughsawn hardwoods—a 4/4 plank is 1 in. thick before milling. The finished dimensions of the doors and fronts will be less, but 5/4 planks still end up being about ¼ in. thicker than 4/4 planks.) I like to use the thicker wood because the fronts won't look unusually thin at the edges after the profile is milled (see

the photo at the top of this page). And when it comes time to attach the drawer fronts with screws into the back of the plank, the extra thickness allows more purchase for fasteners.

DOOR PULLS

Cabinet doors and drawers don't really need knobs or handles— you could just grope around the edges, get a finger hold, and pull them open—but some sort of hardware pull will make the task much easier. It's amazing what even the simplest of pulls will do to dress up and finish off a kitchen. Among the elements of cabinet style, opening hardware is a major player.

There are many different styles of knobs and handles on the market (see the photo above) and just as many opinions about what looks good. I have my personal preferences, but my professional policy is to steer clear of the hardware selection process. I tell customers to shop around until they find knobs or handles that they like, and then I install them. That's the advice I offer you here—except that I'll show you how to install the hardware yourself in Chapter 8.

As for whether you should use all knobs, or all handles, or a combination of knobs on drawers and handles on doors, or vice-versa, there are no rules that I know of. It's done every way, so, again, just do what looks good to you.

There is one little bit of hardware advice I'd like to offer, though, and that is to consider using decorative metal backer plates (see the photo above right). They are an extra expense, they're not available for all knob or handle styles, and you might not like the way they look, but they do serve a practical purpose. Backer plates protect the door around the pull from fingernail scratches that can wear away the finish over time.

If you decide not to use knobs or handles, two options you should be aware of are routed finger pulls and continuous wood pulls (CWPs). Routed finger pulls are nothing more than a routed recess on the back edge of a door rail. They make the grope-and-open approach easier, but I don't recommend this type of pull with wood doors because it leads to premature wear on the face frame around the pull (fingernails again). CWPs (see the drawing at right) are a more sensible choice because, the way they're designed, those dreadful fingernails don't do any visible damage.

Backer plates are seldom used, but they are a practical item because they protect the wood around the knob or pull from fingernail wear over time.

CONTINUOUS WOOD PULLS

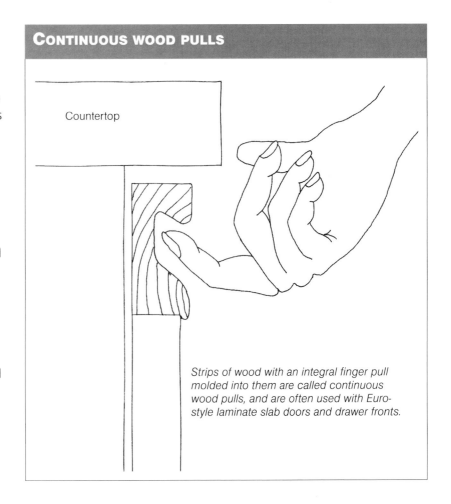

Countertop

Strips of wood with an integral finger pull molded into them are called continuous wood pulls, and are often used with Euro-style laminate slab doors and drawer fronts.

Traditional hinges are the most common style used when refacing cabinets with traditional overlay doors. These variable-overlay hinges are available with several finishes.

HINGES

If you use full-overlay or traditional-overlay doors with hidden hinges, that's a simple style decision. But with overlay doors having traditional face-frame-mounted hinges, a portion of the hinge is clearly visible, and that means you have more style choices to consider.

The design of traditional cabinet hinges most often used in refacing is basic and fairly universal (see the photo above). A plate (door wing) attaches to the back of the door with three screws. The pin and knuckles (pivot point) of the hinge rest against the outside edge of the door, and a decorative mounting section (frame wing) attaches to the cabinet face frame with two screws.

There are minor variations in mounting-plate designs, but the major style differences are in the colors of the hinges. Solid brass hinges are available, but they're quite expensive and rarely used. Plated-steel hinges are widely available, with finishes ranging from polished, burnished, and antique to black, white, gray, copper, and chrome.

Almost all my traditional-overlay refacing is done using burnished brass hinges because the color is subtle and blends in with most door styles. I don't like hinges to stand out, but some people choose bright brass hinges to complement bright brass pulls, and they end up looking good.

VALANCES

A valance is a piece of wood finished to match the cabinets and is usually fitted between two separate sections of wall cabinets (see the photo above). The most common location is between cabinets that flank a window. Although not absolutely necessary, the valance visually connects the two groups of cabinets, and it serves a practical purpose by providing some cover for lighting.

If your kitchen can be improved by adding a valance, do it. If you already have one or more of them, they can, in most instances, be resurfaced with veneer, but I don't recommend it. I prefer to replace valances using solid wood—it makes for a better job, and it also gives you a chance to change the style (see the drawing on p. 30). The most basic valances are straight boards, and sometimes a straight valance is all that's needed. For a touch

This kitchen has a distinctive valance design that provides a little custom touch. Prior to refacing, the cabinets were birch plywood; the new doors are cherry with a medium-dark stain.

Valances can range from a basic straight board to intricate patterns.

of detail, you can have a molded profile routed along the bottom edge. From there, anything goes.

SOFFITS

In kitchen parlance, the soffit is the space between the ceiling and the top of the wall cabinets. Strictly speaking, the soffit is not part of the cabinets, but it does affect molding choices, as well as overall style. Soffit styles can be divided into four categories (see the drawing on the facing page): open, closed flush, closed with a slight overhang, and closed with an extended overhang.

If you like your soffit the way it is, then don't mess with it. But if you want to change it, now's the time. Be aware that if you want to open an existing

closed soffit, you will probably have to spackle and repaint the ceiling (assuming it's drywall). It's likely you'll encounter little surprises like electrical wires, plumbing pipes, and/or heating ducts that have been conveniently concealed there.

Closing an open soffit is something I do more often, and it's a great idea if you want to eliminate the baskets, bowls, and other dust-collecting clutter that is usually stashed on top of the cabinets. A closed soffit also gives the kitchen more of a custom look. When closing an open soffit, I almost always opt for the closed-flush style because it's very easy to do (on pp. 102-103 you'll learn how) and looks just fine.

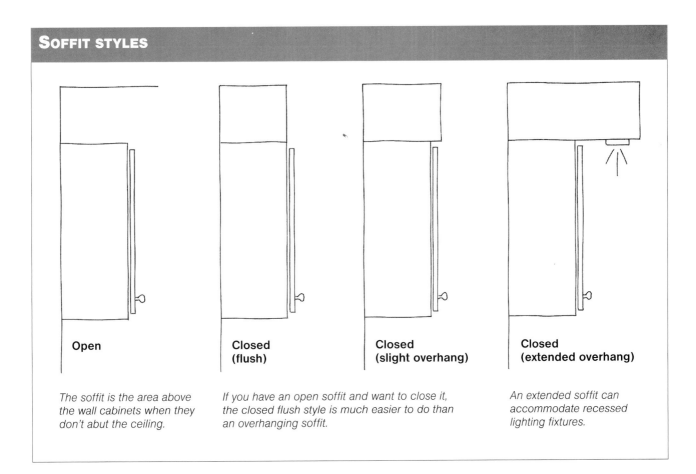

Open

Closed (flush)

Closed (slight overhang)

Closed (extended overhang)

The soffit is the area above the wall cabinets when they don't abut the ceiling.

If you have an open soffit and want to close it, the closed flush style is much easier to do than an overhanging soffit.

An extended soffit can accommodate recessed lighting fixtures.

MOLDINGS

Like valances and frame-and-panel door designs, moldings have limitless style possibilities. Some moldings cover up cracks, or the joints where two different materials meet; others are purely decorative. The drawing on p. 32 shows the moldings most often added or replaced when refacing.

Toe kicks (the recessed bottom parts of base cabinets) can be covered with wood or laminate to match the cabinets. Wood is not a very practical choice in an area that will probably get banged into with brooms, mops, and feet, but it looks nice, and a lot of people want it. For wood toe kicks, I use prefinished strips of $1/4$-in. plywood (the same material used on cabinet sides) or solid wood, followed up with a matching quarter-round or base shoe (also called shoe molding). Base shoe can continue around the side of the cabinets and the exposed back sides of islands and peninsulas. Glued-on vinyl base is a more durable toe-kick cover than plywood, although some people consider it ugly. It comes in basic black and a variety of colors so you can match the floor. Tile on the toe kick (with a tile floor) is another sensible option.

A molding around the bottom of the wall cabinets is an option that you may want to consider (see the photos on p. 35). This molding detail is easy to apply, and the effect is very nice—it also serves as a valance to shield under-cabinet lighting.

Cove or crown molding

Molding that covers juncture of cabinets and soffit

Molding at bottom of upper cabinets

Toe-kick cover: plywood, vinyl, or tile

Base shoe (used with wood-covered toe kicks)

At the top of the cabinets, where they either end (open soffit) or meet the ceiling or a closed soffit, is another logical place for a molding. An open soffit doesn't necessarily need a molding, but a galley rail or crown molding can really make it look spiffy. With closed soffits having an overhang, no molding is necessary unless you do a poor job at butting the laminate or veneer up to the soffit. If that happens, a small square or quarter-round strip will solve the problem. With closed flush soffits, a simple inconspicuous strip, rectangular in cross section, can be used to cover the joint between the cabinet and the soffit.

RELATIVE COSTS OF DIFFERENT STYLES

Thus far, I've mentioned very little about the cost of refacing a kitchen, and that's because I think it's a good idea for you to decide first what you like, regardless of price. Then, if necessary, you can make style changes to meet the budget. You may find that you can have exactly what you want for less than you thought, especially if you're doing the work yourself.

In a book of this sort, it's impossible to give precise information about costs. Kitchens differ in size, and style variations are virtually limitless. Moreover, material costs can vary widely depending on the supplier, and the price of hardwood is notoriously volatile. Should you hire someone to do the work, you'll have to factor in the cost of that person's labor too. What I can offer you are some general guidelines about the relative costs of one style decision over another.

In terms of wood species, oak costs less than cherry and usually also a bit less than maple. Curiously, pine doors cost about the same as oak. If you want cherry but think it will be way out of your price range, you might be surprised to find that the total difference is not all that much.

You also have to look at lumber grades when you look at costs. Some door suppliers use only Select woods but most offer a choice of different grades, and the price varies accordingly. If you intend to have a clear or washed finish, you should definitely spring for the better wood; even if you don't, it's not a bad idea to get better wood. As you might expect, suppliers who finish doors (some don't) charge less for unfinished doors than for finished ones. Washes cost extra.

In terms of door styles, the more involved the production process is and the more solid wood used in the door, the higher the cost will be. A simple slab door is the least expensive option. Laminate slabs cost a bit more, and laminate slabs with continuous wood pulls cost even more. Simple styles of flat-panel doors (including arches) are next, followed by plank doors, and square raised panels—the latter two are roughly equivalent in price. Raised-panel doors climb steadily in price as you add a top arch, bottom arch, and multiple panels. Mitered frames cost more than butted mortise-and-tenon frames. Frame-only doors cost about as much as basic flat-panel doors, and the price goes up proportionately with the number of mullioned sections. High-quality RTF raised-panels units cost almost as much as oak raised panels.

Corresponding drawer-front prices relate as you might expect: Slabs are the least expensive, followed by basic square planks, raised planks, raised planks of 5/4 stock, and, finally, frame and raised panel.

For knobs and handles, prices range from less than $1 to more than $50. Most are from $3 to $5. If you look in the right places (see Resources on pp. 155-157) you can get solid-brass pulls for a reasonable price.

Hinges vary in price too, though not as much as pulls. Hidden cup hinges cost two to three times as much as basic burnished-brass traditional hinges. If the door maker drills the cup holes in the door for you, that's an added expense. Traditional hinges other than burnished brass cost a little more money; solid brass costs a lot more.

Valances and moldings are like doors. The more complicated the design, the more money they cost.

BEFORE

When I was a greenhorn carpenter, I borrowed $10,000 and used it to build my own house. That wasn't a whole lot of money to work with, but I kept the plan small, used some salvaged materials, and did all the work myself. When it came to the kitchen, I didn't know diddly about design or cabinet construction, but I still managed to put together a functional plan and inexpensive (but solidly constructed) cabinets that were at least presentable. That was 15 years ago, and I still live in the house. I had done almost nothing to improve or update the kitchen since I built it. However, when I started writing this book, I realized that I needed a well-worn kitchen to photograph the refacing process in, My old kitchen (see the photos at left) was the perfect candidate.

The style and design decisions I made reflect my family's lifestyle, just as your decisions will. My wife, Marlene, and I have three young children. We live in the country, rarely entertain, and don't prepare extravagant meals, though my wife does bake bread regularly and also cans and freezes produce from the garden. In addition, she home schools our kids, so she's very busy. I'm wrapped up in my work, so I'm busy too. And our kids, you know they're busy. What this all boils down to is that we wanted a kitchen that would be efficient, well organized, and easy to work in—convenience was the key word. And we wanted the room to look good, too.

The Kimball kitchen before refacing was humble but serviceable. This built-in kitchen with birch-plywood doors was never completely finished, looked bland, and was well worn. It was time for a change.

With cabinet style in mind, Marlene and I decided that we wanted the warmth and character of natural wood. Although we love the look of cherry, we decided on oak because of its greater durability. Oak also happens to be readily available in good grades, which is important to me since I decided to make my own doors. For a finish, we decided on clear.

For a door style, we opted for double-flat panels—a classic design that's easy to make. There are no inside and outside profiles on the door frame, nor is there any applied molding; everything is squared off. We added a valance over the sink, where there had been none before. The valance and drawer fronts are basic flat planks. Our choice of opening hardware was simple white ceramic knobs and hidden cup hinges; the existing traditional style of visible cabinet face frames was changed to a full-overlay style. The soffit remained closed.

While I was at it, I made a few cabinet modifications to improve kitchen efficiency (see pp. 52-53). And for changes unrelated to the cabinetry, I built a new plastic-laminate countertop, added ceramic tile on the walls, updated some of the appliances, put better general lighting in the ceiling (already done in the "before" photos), and installed a new vinyl floor. We achieved our style and design objectives with a limited budget (about $1,500 for the refacing materials), and I expect to get more years out of this kitchen than I did from the old one.

AFTER

The refaced kitchen features shop-made oak double-flat-panel doors in the full-overlay style and a new valance over the sink. Appliances, flooring, and countertops were upgraded at the same time as well.

CE REMODELING
FOR EFFICIENCY

As the last chapter showed, refacing can make a huge improvement in the overall appearance of your old cabinets, but that's not all. Refacing also provides you with an opportunity to improve the efficiency of your existing kitchen. If you modify the old cabinetry, add a few new cabinets, or install new appliances, the beauty of your refaced kitchen will be more than skin deep, and the room can become a more pleasant and productive place to work in.

EXISTING CABINETS

Efficient function, as it relates to cabinets, can mean different things to different people, but it all boils down to one word: organization. Some people organize with the idea that they want to fit as much as they can into a cabinet; never mind that they have to remove half the contents to get to the waffle iron when they need it. Most of us, however, define efficient function as organization with accessibility. That's the ultimate challenge.

Begin your quest for an organized kitchen by getting rid of the clutter—by clutter I mean the things that you use rarely, if ever. Do you really need that fondue set? Or the glass froster? Maybe so, but probably not. If you

can't bear to part with such treasures outright, you could pack them in a box, put it in the attic, and free up some valuable cabinet space. Your cabinets will need to be completely cleaned out anyway when you do the refacing, so it's a perfect opportunity to take a hard look at the stuff you've stashed away over the years.

When you've reduced your inventory of kitchen gadgets to a more manageable size, think about where you'll be putting these items away and how you'll be putting them away once the refacing is done. Where to put things away is pretty much common sense—you put them near where they'll be needed. For example, everyday glasses and dishes should be stored near the sink or dishwasher, cooking pans near the stove, staples such as flour and sugar near the food-preparation area. Obviously, it would not be a good organizational move to store your everyday silverware in a cabinet over the refrigerator. How to put things away is a more interesting subject. With just a few small remodeling improvements, the overall organization of your kitchen and your ease of access to the equipment stored therein can be greatly improved.

Shelves, drawers, and slide-out trays

Kitchen cabinets can be modified in various ways to improve their efficiency; see the drawing on p. 38 for some examples. Many wall and base cabinets have two doors that meet at a mullion, or center dividing stile. On cabinets up to around 32 in. wide, the mullion can usually be removed without creating a structural problem. This opens up the cabinet and allows you to store bigger items in it. When the new doors are put on, they are sized to meet with a 1/8-in. space between them. Similarly, two small side-by-side drawers can be changed to one wide drawer by removing the divider and making a new drawer.

When it comes to drawers, there are plenty of opportunities for improvement. First, if the existing drawers are made of wood and they're broken or worn, they should, of course, be repaired. It's normal for joints to weaken with age and use, and bottoms often sag and loosen under heavy loads. I've given new life to many old, but still serviceable, drawers by knocking them apart and regluing and screwing them together, and replacing the bottom if needed.

Old drawers can also be completely replaced. If they're made of molded plastic, replacement is definitely a good idea. If they're made of particleboard and are still in good shape, reuse them if you want, but particleboard drawers that are broken are seldom worth repairing. You can make your own new drawer boxes or buy custom made drawers or Ready To Assemble (RTA) drawer boxes (see pp. 85-86 for more about the latter two options).

Like drawers, old drawer slides can also be repaired or replaced. Although you can still get parts for most older styles of slides from mail-order suppliers or in well-stocked hardware stores, I recommend switching to the popular Euro-style side-mount drawer slides instead. These slides consist of rails that are L-shaped in cross section and fit along the side and bottom on each side of the drawer. The slides operate very smoothly and can support heavier drawer loads than the older types of slides. Although it takes a little finesse to install these new slides properly in face-frame cabinets (see pp. 145-146), they will give trouble-free service for many years.

Kitchen efficiency can sometimes be improved by adding or removing drawers. For example, a standard base cabinet with one drawer on top and a door underneath can be converted to a base cabinet with three or four drawers by fitting in some rails before refacing and installing the new drawers. Conversely, an existing base cabinet with all drawers (called a drawer base in the trade) can be made into a storage unit for large items (a door base) by getting rid of some or all of the drawers and rails and simply putting a door on the opening. Convoluted arrangements of drawers within one cabinet can also be simplified into a more visually pleasing and efficient design.

If your cabinets currently have fixed shelves (wall cabinets in particular), you might want to remove those shelves and put in adjustable shelving standards and brackets to accommodate the items you want to put in there. You can reinstall the same shelves or new ones, if the old ones didn't come out in one piece. If you

Eliminate central dividers

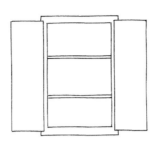

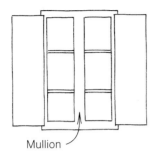

Mullion

On cabinets with doors or drawers that meet at a center mullion), the mullion can be removed to allow unobstructed access to the contents.

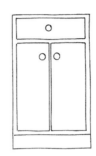

Two small drawers can be replaced with one wide drawer.

Change doors to drawers, or the reverse

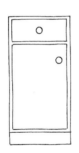

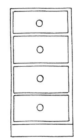

By removing or installing rail pieces, existing cabinet face frames can be altered to gain or eliminate drawers— whichever suits your storage needs.

Simplify convoluted arrangements

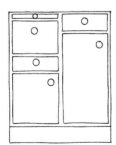

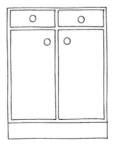

The cabinet at far left has a choppy mix of three drawers, two doors, and a pull- out cutting board. By modifying the face frame, you can turn it into a more visually pleasing piece, more in keeping with standard cabinetry.

already have adjustable shelving but it's thin and has sagged, now is the time to put in some sturdy new shelves of ¾-in. plywood. You might also consider installing an additional shelf if it fits and it suits your needs.

Slide-out shelves (see the photo at right) are an excellent organizational upgrade for base cabinets. They are essentially drawer boxes without fronts that are placed behind the door. Slide-out shelves are not as convenient as drawers because you have to open the cabinet door before sliding them out, but they provide very easy access to items that would normally be buried back inside the cabinet. Slide-out shelving is also handy in pantry cabinets.

Sink cabinets don't have upper drawers because the sink is in the way, so they have an attached front without the drawer—it's called a false front. Nowadays it's popular to attach hinges to the front and install a small flip-down tray on the back (see the top photo on p. 40). It's handy for storing unsightly but useful sink clutter such as scouring pads and scrub brushes.

Trash bins are another kitchen essential—they aren't pretty to look at, but you need to get at them easily. Under the sink is a perfect location. For another slide-out convenience, you can position a trash bin on a slide mechanism; open the door and the container can be easily slid out. One brand of slide-out hardware pulls the trash bin out automatically when you open the door (see the bottom photo on p. 40). Another approach is to fit the trash bin into a framework, attach it to the back of the door, and, with the aid of a heavy-duty drawer slide, have the door open straight out like a drawer, as shown in the top drawing on p. 41.

Wide slide-out shelves in cabinets that don't have a dividing stile provide very convenient access to what's stored inside.

Hardware kits for a variety of different styles and sizes of slide-out trash receptacles are readily available at some home centers and from mail-order suppliers, a couple of which are listed in Resources on pp. 155-157. Concealed garbage-type receptacles can also be used for storage of recyclables. Some recycling units have four smaller plastic containers on one slide-out mechanism, and there are also multi-container recycling units made to fit in a lazy-Susan corner cabinet. Mail-order sources also offer a host of other clever cabinet organizers, such as pull-out cup racks, roll-out wire vegetable bins, cutlery organizers, and spice racks. The choices are too numerous to mention here, but they are well worth considering.

Small trays located behind a false front in a sink base cabinet can squeak a little storage space out of what would otherwise be a dead area.

Lazy Susans

Revolving shelves, commonly known as lazy Susans (why, I don't know), have been and continue to be a popular kitchen organizational option. They are typically found in base corner cabinets, where they make good use of what would otherwise be a blind corner (see the bottom drawing on the facing page). Lazy Susans can have full-round shelves with a hinged door, pie-cut shelves with an attached inset door (it spins around with the shelving), or kidney-shaped shelves with a a hinged overlay bifold door that swings out (see the drawing on p. 42).

Most lazy Susans pivot on a post, but many pie-cut shelves have an odd top-mounted pivot mechanism and no center post. When I first started refacing cabinets, I encountered a kitchen that had two pie-cut lazy Susan units with "post-less" pivots. Unbeknownst to me, they were worn out. Although I did notice that the doors rubbed badly on the face frame and turned hard, I figured I just needed to tighten up or readjust something. It was

This trash bin is out of sight under the sink. It pulls out automatically when the door is opened.

A SLIDE-OUT TRASH BIN

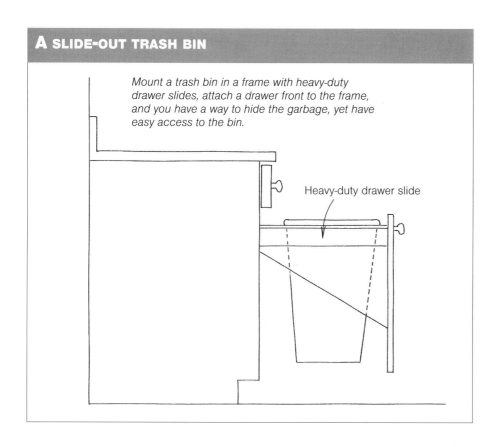

Mount a trash bin in a frame with heavy-duty drawer slides, attach a drawer front to the frame, and you have a way to hide the garbage, yet have easy access to the bin.

Heavy-duty drawer slide

BLIND CORNER

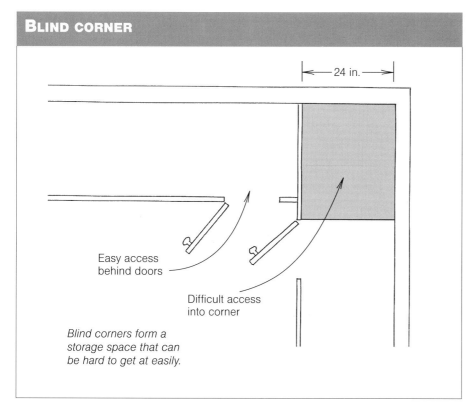

|← 24 in. →|

Easy access behind doors

Difficult access into corner

Blind corners form a storage space that can be hard to get at easily.

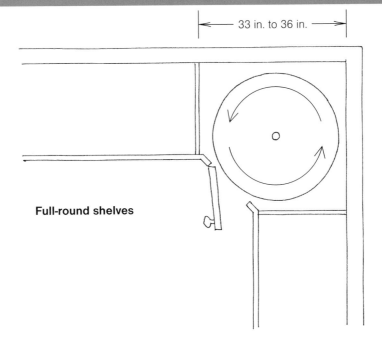

|← 33 in. to 36 in. →|

Lazy Susans eliminate blind corners, but they require 33 in. to 36 in. of wall space.

Full-round shelves

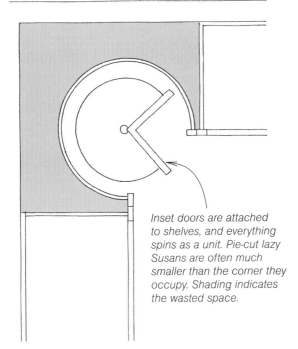

Pie-cut shelves

Inset doors are attached to shelves, and everything spins as a unit. Pie-cut lazy Susans are often much smaller than the corner they occupy. Shading indicates the wasted space.

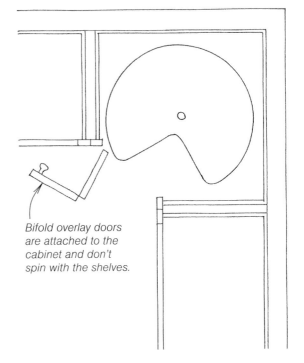

Kidney-shaped shelves

Bifold overlay doors are attached to the cabinet and don't spin with the shelves.

not so. The job turned out to be a nightmare. After putting the refaced doors on, I spent several frustrating hours getting them to turn freely and fit evenly in the opening. In the end, I had to settle for a crooked door fit. The customer didn't seem to mind (the shelves hadn't even worked before), but it was a lazy Susan epiphany for me. Since that job, I've changed my approach to pie-cut lazy Susans. Now I rip them out, install new kidney-shaped shelves with a center-post pivot, and put a bifold overlay door on the opening. I recommend you do the same (for instructions, see pp. 96-97) because, for one thing, it ensures that you will have a properly operating lazy Susan for the next 20 years. Besides that, changing to an overlay door style means the formerly inset doors will then match the overlay style on the rest of the kitchen.

If you already have a full-round lazy Susan, it has a center-post pivot. If it's an older model with plywood shelves, the pivot mechanism probably consists of a sturdy metal post with a bottom-mounted pivot stud that rides on a metal bearing plate, and it's likely that the whole thing still works decently. If so, you may only need to lubricate it with some grease at the pivot point (under the bottom shelf). If, when you do this, you notice that you probably should have done it ten years ago (lots of wear and metal filings in the area), don't feel bad because hardly anyone in the world knows (or even cares) that old-style center-post lazy Susans should be lubricated on occasion. Depending on how bad the wear is and whether or not you can find a replacement pivot, you might just want to chuck the whole unit and

upgrade to one of the better-quality plastic-shelf lazy Susans on the market; they work more smoothly and don't need regular maintenance. (For information on ordering lazy Susans, see pp. 87-88.)

If your kitchen has a blind corner and you'd like to install a lazy Susan there, it might be possible, but more often than not, there won't be enough room (from the back wall, a lazy Susan requires 33 in. to 36 in. of space in each direction). The sink placement or some other restriction makes the plan impractical, if not impossible. What else can you do to improve access to a blind corner? Not much, but there are a couple of options (see the drawing on p. 44).

If the blind corner happens to be part of a peninsula, you can simply cut an opening from the back side and install some doors and shelving or a row of drawers. Access wouldn't be directly from the kitchen side, but you would still gain easy access to some valuable storage space.

The other option is to install a blind-corner shelving system. Blind-corner shelves are accessed from a door adjacent to the blind corner. When you open the the door, two semicircular shelves, positioned partly in the blind corner and partly in the door opening, pivot out. Better-quality units pivot and then slide out for even better accessibility to the shelving contents. It's a nifty setup, but the problem with blind-corner shelving is that the shelves also take up an otherwise usable section of cabinet behind the door, and they aren't really all that big. The way I see it, the shelves are as much of a loss as they are a gain.

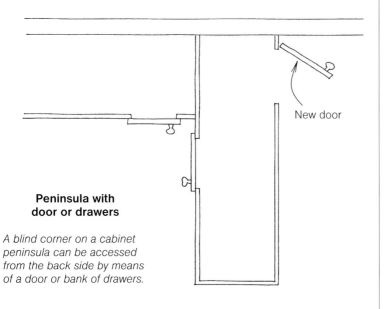

New door

**Peninsula with
door or drawers**

*A blind corner on a cabinet
peninsula can be accessed
from the back side by means
of a door or bank of drawers.*

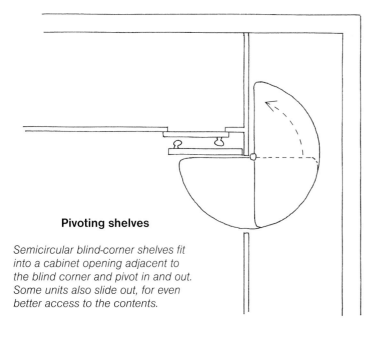

Pivoting shelves

*Semicircular blind-corner shelves fit
into a cabinet opening adjacent to
the blind corner and pivot in and out.
Some units also slide out, for even
better access to the contents.*

Sometimes it's just impossible to make a blind corner easily accessible. When that proves to be the case, it's as good a place as any to stash the fondue set.

NEW CABINETS

If your kitchen has the necessary room, the most obvious way to gain more storage space is by installing a few additional cabinets. Extra cabinetry could include some wall and/or base units or a section of island cabinetry (see the sidebar on the facing page). Broom and pantry cabinets are other popular additions. The dual advantage of additional base cabinets is that you'll gain countertop space too.

When adding new cabinets, you have three choices. You can buy brand-new stock cabinets from a home center, reuse salvaged cabinets, or make new ones yourself. If you can locate some decent salvaged cabinetry, that's definitely a great way to go (see the sidebar on p. 46). Cabinet refacing itself is essentially a form of recycling. And whether you recycle the cabinets already in your kitchen or cabinets salvaged from someone else's kitchen (someone who doesn't choose the reface route) doesn't really matter, because when the job is all done, nobody will know the difference. So if you need a few extra cabinets to complete your refacing plans and your brother-in-law just tore his out when he had his kitchen remodeled and some of his cabinets will work for you, see if he'll donate them to the cause. When he sees his grungy old cabinets with a fresh new refacing, he won't believe his eyes (and when you tell him how much money you saved with refacing, he won't believe his ears).

Islands seem to be on everybody's kitchen wish list, and for good reason. A centrally located counter and cabinet can indeed be a real boon to efficient kitchen operation. However, not all kitchens are big enough to accommodate an island. Some, like my own kitchen, which is 9 ft. by 10 ft., are obviously too small, but in many others it's a close call. I often encounter people who sincerely want an island in their layout but really don't have the room to make it work the way it should.

I'm not going to be the one to say you can't have that kitchen island you've dreamed about for years, but I do want you to be aware of the critical measurements used by kitchen planning specialists when integrating an island into a kitchen layout (see the drawing below). In a one-cook kitchen, a 42-in. clearance between cabinets is the key distance to keep in mind when deciding if there is sufficient floor space to accommodate an island. Anything less is a compromise. Don't go below 33 in. unless the area is used primarily as a passageway—and if that's the case, 30 in. is the absolute minimum.

If you have any doubts about the feasibility of a plan, outline the proposed island area with masking tape on the floor to get a better idea of clearances and how they will affect your kitchen efficiency. Better yet, get some big pieces of cardboard and tape them together into a full-size island mock-up. Put a cardboard top piece on and use it for a few days.

Size and clearance recommendations

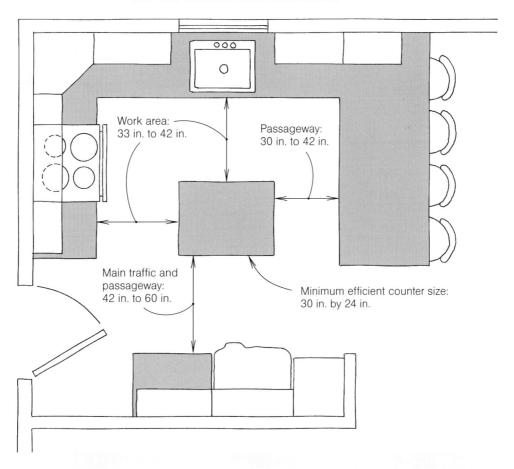

Work area: 33 in. to 42 in.

Passageway: 30 in. to 42 in.

Main traffic and passageway: 42 in. to 60 in.

Minimum efficient counter size: 30 in. by 24 in.

The third option, making the cabinets yourself, has several advantages. First, you can build them in place, which is sometimes easier than building them in the shop and installing them later, particularly with base cabinets. Second, you can easily size your cabinets to accommodate odd requirements (which are not at all unusual in older built-in kitchens). For example, stock cabinets are typically made in widths starting at 9 in. and increasing to 42 in. in 3-in. increments, and they come only in standard depths and heights. If you need something like a 19¾-in.-wide wall cabinet that is 31 in. high and 11½ in. deep, you won't find a stock cabinet to fit the bill, but you can make one that size as easily as any other.

Making your own cabinets doesn't have to be a big deal, and in most cases I would recommend it, even if you've never built a cabinet before. This is a perfect opportunity to get your feet wet, because cabinets that are going to be refaced don't have to be constructed with the same precision and expense that would otherwise be needed (see the sidebar on the facing page).

There are times, however, when you will be better off just buying a new cabinet. Once I had a customer who wanted a standard-size pantry cabinet with an elaborate and specific arrangement of fold-out and revolving shelves (she showed me a picture from some cabinet sales literature). I didn't have the time or inclination to make such a

SALVAGED CABINETS

If you don't have any cabinets at all in your kitchen or if the ones you have are ratty beyond repair, it's entirely possible to collect old cabinets from one or more sources and mix them together to come up with a decent layout in your kitchen. And if you're a natural scrounger, you'll love the challenge of filling your kitchen with functional castoff cabinets that won't cost you a cent.

Even if scrounging doesn't work out, you should be able to get what you need for next to nothing. My local newspaper carries classified ads for building materials, and many times I've noticed people trying to unload their old cabinets there. Look under the "miscellaneous" listing too. You can often get leads on kitchens that are going to be torn out from retail

cabinet stores and remodeling contractors. Don't contact such sources just once; check with them frequently.

In my own work as a kitchen remodeler, I've torn out many decent cabinets. Sometimes they have gone directly to the landfill; other times, my customers have either given them away or sold them for less than $100. I certainly wouldn't pay more than that for a bunch of cabinets unless they were in exceptionally good shape and I could use almost all of them.

If you really want to save some money on used cabinetry, don't be too anxious. Let the word get out, keep your eyes open, and you'll find a great deal.

unit, so I bought the cabinet she showed me (with the least expensive door style), discarded the doors, installed the cabinet, and refaced it to match the rest of the kitchen. I was able to do all this for less money than if I had made the pantry myself. This brings up an important point—any cabinet made by a professional crafts-man is probably going to cost a customer more than an average stock cabinet would. However, that's not

likely to be the case when you make your own cabinets—sweat equity makes a big difference.

NEW APPLIANCES

People expect their kitchen appliances to increase kitchen efficiency, and that's what they usually do. Sometimes, though, having too many small appliances can become a hin-drance to efficient countertop organization. That's why a lot of them are designed to be mounted under wall cabinets, where they're out of the

QUICK CUSTOM CABINETS

Making new kitchen cabinets that will be refaced does not require anywhere near the experience and skill needed to make cabinets that won't be refaced. Since the face frames will be veneered and plywood skins will cover the exposed cabinet ends, it's perfectly acceptable to use the most basic of joinery tech-niques and fasten components together using visible nails and screws. Salvaged lumber can also be utilized.

Cabinetmaking purists may cringe at the idea, but good kitchen cabinets can be fabri-cated without milling dadoes and grooves and rabbets. That's not to say that if you cobble together a piece of junk, refacing will make it all okay in the end. Cabinets still need to be built square and sturdy, but as long as those requirements are met, the rest of the work needn't be fussy.

When I build new cabinets that will be refaced, I use $3/4$-in. birch plywood for the sides, bottoms,

tops, and shelves. For the backs I normally use $1/4$-in. birch ply-wood. Before assembling any of the pieces, I spray-finish them with a water-based polyurethane. Sides are fastened to tops and bottoms with basic butt joints and drywall screws. The $3/4$-in. ply-wood provides ample wood for anchoring into, though a pilot hole for the screws is usually nec-essary to prevent splitting. I often use biscuits in conjunction with glue and screws to make the con-nection; the screws (positioned between the biscuits) do away with the need for any clamps, and make a secure attachment on their own.

Cabinet backs get nailed on with 1-in. ring-shank nails, and face-frame pieces are fastened with glue and nails or screws. For face-frame material, I use leftover strips of $3/4$-in. plywood or com-mon pine. The face frames need not be assembled before they're fastened to the cabinet; the indi-vidual pieces can be fastened on directly. Any unevenness at the

butt joints where rails and stiles meet can be leveled off with a belt sander after the glue dries.

That, in a nutshell, is my approach to making reface cabinets. It's a fast and easy method that gives you solidly made cabinets, and when the job is done, it looks great. You may, of course, use whatever cabinetmaking approach you feel comfortable with. For books on cabinet-making in general, see Further Reading on p. 159.

Making individual cabinet units and then fastening them in place is only one way to build kitchen cabinets. The other is to build them right in place. Built-in kitchens were common in the 1950s and 1960s. If your existing cabinets are built-ins and you want to add on or modify them, you can certainly copy the joinery and construction techniques used in the originals. If you can make improvements such as using screws instead of nails, do it.

way, yet convenient to use. Major appliances—dishwashers, microwaves, and stoves—are often an important part of reface remodeling plans. Because these appliances are generally built in, they call for more planning in terms of their requirements.

Dishwashers

If your kitchen lacks a built-in dishwasher and you really want one, you'll need to give up a 24-in.-wide section of base cabinets; that's how wide the appliance typically is. If you have the space, the dishwasher should be placed immediately adjacent to the sink, but in a cramped kitchen, you may have to put it elsewhere. Try to position the unit as close to the sink as possible, but not so close that the opened door of the appliance restricts your movement, either around the sink or while loading and unloading dishes.

Keep in mind that dishwashers will need a hot-water supply line and a drain. These connections can usually be made by hooking the dishwasher's supply pipe and drain hose into the supply pipe and drain line under the kitchen sink. Power supply is another consideration. A separate (dedicated) electrical circuit is recommended. Refer to the dishwasher's instruction sheet and local building codes for specifics on electrical and plumbing hook-ups.

Microwave ovens

In the last decade, microwave ovens have become standard kitchen fixtures because of the incredible convenience they provide. If you have an older kitchen, chances are the microwave isn't built in. It probably dominates a section of countertop or sits out off to the side on a cart. Refacing provides you with an opportunity to integrate the microwave into your kitchen plans.

One way to do this is to build a microwave cabinet up off the counter to hold the microwave you now have (see the top photo on p. 34). An arrangement like this will free up some countertop workspace and put the appliance at a convenient operating height, but you'll lose some cabinet storage space, and that's counterproductive. A better approach is to buy a new microwave that's designed to be mounted over the range and install it there. I do this quite often when refacing, and it works out great.

Over-the-range microwaves fit into a space that's 30 in. wide. This is the standard width of most range hoods with exhaust fans. If you have an exhaust fan over your range, you will need to remove it. These microwaves have a built-in exhaust fan that will either recirculate air through a charcoal filter or exhaust it into an exterior vent at the top or in the back (usually the same vent that the old exhaust fan used). The new microwaves have a light on the bottom to illuminate the stove top.

Unit heights and recommended clearances for microwaves may vary from manufacturer to manufacturer, but most built-in microwaves are about 15 in. high. That means they can fit under a wall cabinet that's 15 in. or 18 in. high and still maintain the minimum 15-in. clearance from the stove top (double-check manufacturer's recommendations for proper clearances).

Before refacing (left), this kitchen had room to spare around the stove. The solution? Take up the extra space above the stove and to its right with two new wall cabinets and a built-in microwave (below). A new base cabinet closes the gap between the stove and the refrigerator.

Over-the-range microwaves typically attach to the wall by means of a mounting plate that is screwed into one or more wall studs. Most of the weight of the unit (about 80 lb.) rests on the plate, but two or three machine screws are fit down through the wall cabinet into the top of the microwave and draw it up for a tight fit. Electricity is usually supplied through a dedicated 20-amp outlet located inside the cabinet above; the microwave plugs into it.

Microwaves are 30 in. wide. If your old exhaust fan happens to be an oversized monster, there will be 6 in. or 12 in. of space left unfilled when you put the microwave in. Don't waste your time looking for oversized microwaves; they don't exist. You can sometimes build a small frame on either side and install two false panels. Or you can rebuild one or more adjoining cabinets. If neither of those prospects appeals to you, most microwave manufacturers sell a filler panel kit that will take care of the extra space.

Ovens and ranges

Many older kitchens have a separate wall oven and range top, and, quite often, people want to incorporate the two appliances into one range/oven unit. This usually happens when the appliances have outlived their useful lifespan, which, coincidentally, is often around the time the cabinets need refacing. Oven and range consolidation is easy to do with refacing because the space where the old wall oven was can be converted to a deep pantry cabinet (slide-out shelves would be especially nice). The usually rough-sawn oven cutout can be recut or finished off as needed to make it look

good, then refaced along with the rest of the kitchen (see the photo on the facing page). The base cabinet under the old range top will need to be removed (or cut out if the cabinets are built in) to make space for the new stove, but that's not so difficult; any unsightly reconstruction of the face frames will be covered over during the refacing process when they're veneered. Cutting through the old countertop to provide room for the new appliance will prove difficult if you intend to keep the counter and want it to look good, so a new countertop might be in order (see Further Reading on p. 159 for an exceptionally good book on fabricating plastic-laminate countertops). The storage space that is lost from under the range top will be more than made up for by the cabinet or pantry you install where the old wall oven was.

As with other appliances, utility requirements need to be taken into account when installing a stove. In my area, most older ovens and stoves are electric, and people often want to switch to gas. This is, I guess, a good economic move, and it's what may cooks prefer. It's also good because it frees up some extra space in the electrical box for new appliance circuits (which you'll need if you're also installing a microwave or a dishwasher). If you currently have an electric range top and separate oven unit and you combine them into one electric stove, you'll probably find that the existing range-top supply line and breaker will need to be replaced to provide the higher amperage that the newer appliance will require. Check with a qualified electrician on this.

Prior to refacing, this kitchen had a wall oven in the tall cabinet on the left and a range top on the right. The old oven space was filled by a two-door cabinet with adjustable shelves. The range top was replaced by a combination range/oven unit. The new appliance has a downdraft exhaust fan, so the old cooktop fan was replaced with a decorative tile and cherry valance and new lighting behind it.

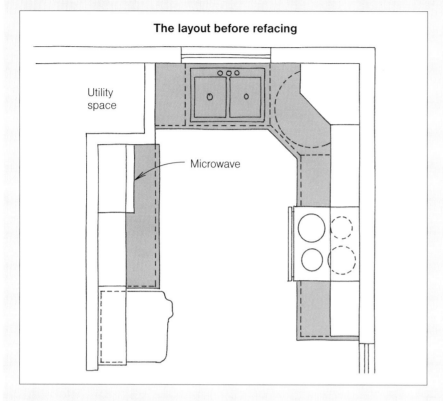

The layout before refacing

Utility space

Microwave

On the base cabinets, I replaced a few cabinet drawers and installed slide-out shelves where I could. On the sink base, the two separate false fronts were unified into one wide front with a tilt tray in each opening. I installed a slide-out trash receptacle behind one sink-base door, too.

Next, I turned my attention to the lazy Susan to the right of the sink. Its three full-round shelves still worked fine after 15 years, and I could have just lubricated the center-post bearing and left it at that, but I decided to install a drawer where the top shelf had been. I also splurged on some clean new shelves. Why? The old plywood shelves didn't have a retaining lip around the edge (plastic units do) and, on occasion, shelf contents would jump ship and jam the works. So I'd have to climb into the cabinet on a search and rescue mission.

NEW CABINETS

I took the wall cabinet that was adjacent to the refrigerator and moved it over where the microwave cabinet had been. Alongside that, I installed a new cabinet that was 10 in. wider than the old microwave cabinet. Putting in the bigger cabinet shifted the refrigerator over to the left just enough for me to cut out the wall behind it and slide the appliance back under the stairs on the other side of the wall. Now the refrigerator almost lines up flush with the front of the base cabinets, and it no longer dominates the kitchen space. To keep small items from falling off the new countertop into the gap between the base cabinet and the refrigerator, I installed a

When I refaced my own kitchen, I incorporated most of the suggestions mentioned in this chapter, and a few others as well. The kitchen in my house is small and relatively efficient for one cook. However, there were many things that my wife, Marlene, and I decided to do to make the space even more efficient. Even though your kitchen plans will be different from mine, you might find it useful to follow along as I explain the changes I made in my kitchen. The before and after drawings show what's being discussed. You may also want to refer to the photos on pp. 34-35.

EXISTING CABINETS

The 12-in.-deep cabinet that was over the refrigerator was reused, but instead of installing it back against the wall, I pulled it out to the front of the 24-in.-deep side panels. This move solved two problems. Junk can no longer accumulate on top of the refrigerator, and the cabinet is much more accessible than it used to be. The clutter and oddball items that had been stored there are now packed away to make room for more important things.

On the wall cabinets, I converted some of the fixed shelves to adjustable shelves. The center mullion on one of the two-door wall cabinets was removed for better accessibility. The two-door wall cabinet to the right of the stove was only 21 in. wide, so I converted it to a single-door cabinet.

refrigerator side panel, which is just a piece of ³/₄-in. plywood with a front trim strip over the edge grain. To finish off the other side of the bulky cooler, I installed a floor-to-ceiling panel, this one with frame-and-panel construction to match the doors. I incorporated a cork board into the top of the side panel and made a new house rule: no more magnets, artwork, or other paper clutter on the front of the fridge.

To the left of the sink, there was a funky two-door (one above the other) base cabinet that served no purpose at all because I never got around to putting a bottom in the top section, so I changed it into a full-height single-door cabinet. I didn't put a drawer in the narrow opening, but now I wish I had because the cabinet looks odd without one.

NEW APPLIANCES AND LIGHTING

Marlene lobbied for a dishwasher, so I fit the appliance in the only logical place I could find, around the corner to the left of the sink. I placed it 18 in. away from the corner because I didn't want the open door to be in the way of a person using the sink. The placement has worked out well.

Our 14-year-old microwave was falling apart and probably leaked radiation, so it was an easy decision to spring for a new over-the-stove microwave. That move alone freed up considerable room for new wall-cabinet space. And it also gave us an exhaust fan where there hadn't been one before (another thing I just never got around to).

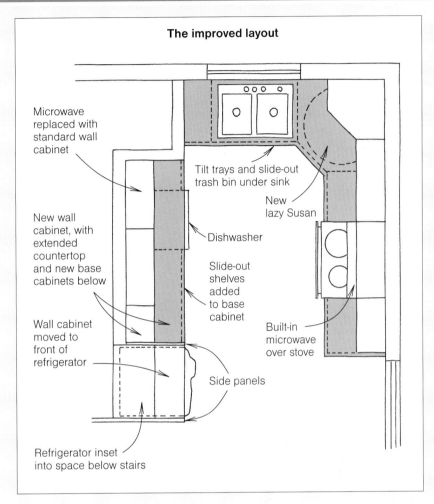

The improved layout

Microwave replaced with standard wall cabinet

Tilt trays and slide-out trash bin under sink

New lazy Susan

New wall cabinet, with extended countertop and new base cabinets below

Dishwasher

Slide-out shelves added to base cabinet

Wall cabinet moved to front of refrigerator

Built-in microwave over stove

Side panels

Refrigerator inset into space below stairs

Another change we made, and one that improved efficiency, was to upgrade the lighting. The old kitchen had only two 60-watt ceiling fixtures, so I replaced them with eight recessed canister lights. To illuminate the countertop directly, I installed small halogen light fixtures under the bottom of the wall cabinets.

THINGS WE HAD TO LIVE WITH

Some things in the kitchen I couldn't change. For example, I would have liked to have the ceiling a few inches higher. And

I would have loved to correct the biggest flaw in the kitchen—that boxed-off area to the left of the sink. Without that obstruction, we could have had more countertop and a true U-shaped kitchen. Unfortunately, that area houses the electrical main-panel box and major drain lines from the bathroom above. So the room isn't perfect; it won't win any prizes. I did the best I could with the space and the resources we had to work with. But isn't that the way it goes with most real-life situations?

3

MEASURING FOR DOORS AND DRAWER FRONTS

Once you've settled on a new kitchen style and design that suits you, it's time to measure your kitchen for the materials you'll need to do the job. I can tell you from experience that many a remodeling project goes awry later because of mistakes made at this stage. Ordering the wrong sizes or not enough of something is not only a discouraging and time-consuming error to rectify, but it also can be costly—especially when dealing with custom-made products like doors. Most cabinet refacers (myself included) have at least a couple of "sample" doors kicking around that were actually left over when they miscalculated the sizes and had to order replacements. On one memorable occasion, I almost got stuck with $1,600 worth of custom-made whitewashed cabinet doors. I had mistakenly specified that the wood be cherry instead of maple. Thankfully, my supplier thought it odd and called to make sure I realized that cherry with a wash would end up looking pink instead of white.

There is always the possibility that you will make mistakes, but this chapter will go a long way toward helping you steer clear of most ordering disasters. I will share with you the system I've

developed to help make sure I order just the right door and drawer-front sizes. The "secret" is to prepare a master drawing of the cabinet fronts and a measurement calculation sheet. Together these two documents will contain all the information you'll need to order new fronts (and other materials as well). They will also serve as a valuable reference when it comes time to do the refacing work.

THE REVEAL REVEALED

I once picked up a brochure on do-it-yourself refacing from a national home-center chain store, and the instructions for measuring doors were essentially to measure the cabinet door openings and add 1 in. to the width and height so the new fronts would overhang the openings 1/2 in. on all sides. That advice is easy and it will usually (though not always) work, but for the best-looking reface job, you will need to put a bit more effort into the task.

In many old kitchens, the spaces between the door and drawer fronts are either not uniform, or they're wider than they need to be, or both. In one kitchen I remodeled, the face frames were all 2 1/4 in. wide and the existing doors overlapped the frame about ¼ in. That meant there was 2 in. of visible face frame around each door, and where two cabinets joined, there was 4 in. of face frame showing; the doors were like islands surrounded by a sea of face frame. If, in that instance, I had merely measured the door openings and added 1 in. to the dimensions, I would have improved the overall appearance of the cabinets only slightly. Instead, I made the doors bigger and the spaces between them smaller.

Those spacings between and around doors and drawer fronts are referred to as reveals. And whether you opt for traditional-overlay or full-overlay Euro-style doors, the reveals will play a key role in how nice your newly refaced kitchen will look. Small reveals are usually more visually appealing than big reveals. If you want a better-than-average refacing job, I encourage you to figure your door sizes with a critical eye toward minimizing reveal spaces and making them as uniform as you possibly can.

MEASURING FOR TRADITIONAL-OVERLAY STYLES

Aesthetics are admittedly subjective, and you can figure any face-frame reveals you want, but for traditional face-frame styles I usually try to aim for the spacings shown in the drawing at right.

Keep in mind when figuring door sizes that inside-corner reveals will need to be bigger than other reveals (see the drawing on the facing page). On base cabinets with adjoining drawers, the drawer on one corner cabinet needs to open without hitting the drawer

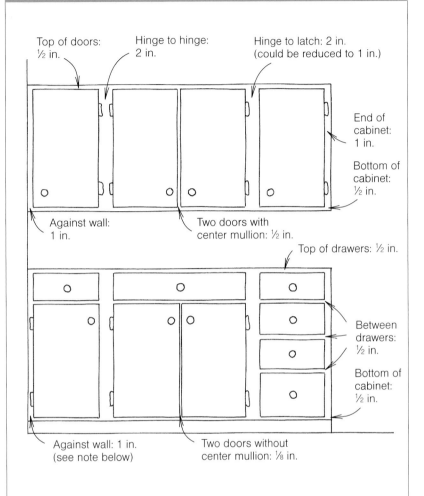

TRADITIONAL OVERLAY: SUGGESTED REVEALS FOR WALL AND BASE CABINETS

Top of doors: ½ in.

Hinge to hinge: 2 in.

Hinge to latch: 2 in. (could be reduced to 1 in.)

End of cabinet: 1 in.

Bottom of cabinet: ½ in.

Against wall: 1 in.

Two doors with center mullion: ½ in.

Top of drawers: ½ in.

Between drawers: ½ in.

Bottom of cabinet: ½ in.

Against wall: 1 in. (see note below)

Two doors without center mullion: ⅛ in.

Note: If a base cabinet with a door hinged against the wall contains slide-out shelves, the reveal should be increased so the door (with pull) can open completely out of the way of the shelves.

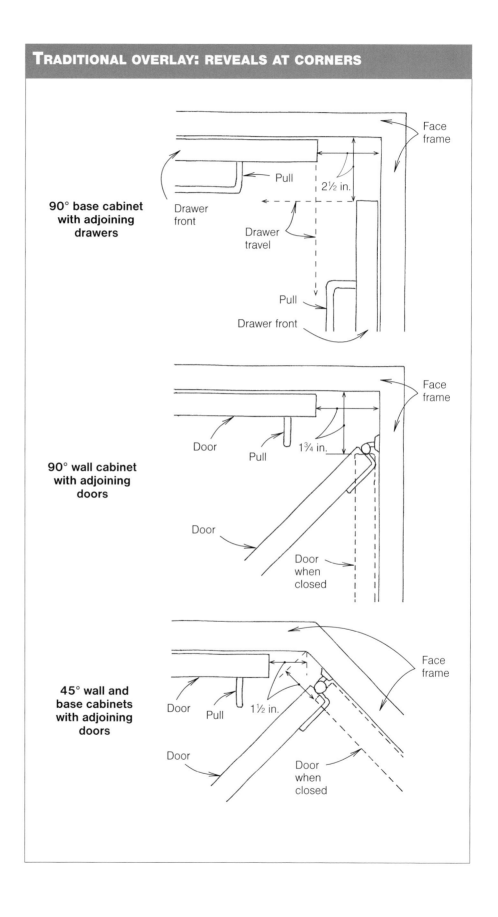

90° base cabinet with adjoining drawers

Face frame

Pull

2½ in.

Drawer front

Drawer travel

Pull

Drawer front

90° wall cabinet with adjoining doors

Face frame

Door

Pull

1¾ in.

Door

Door when closed

45° wall and base cabinets with adjoining doors

Face frame

Door

Pull

1½ in.

Door

Door when closed

Partial-inset drawer front

Variable-overlay drawer front

Pull

Projection difference:
typically about ½ in.

Pull

*If your existing kitchen drawers have a
³⁄₈-in. edge rabbet (partial inset) and you
change them to a variable-overlay style
(as is typically done with refacing), the
new drawers will project about ½ in.
more from the face frame.*

or its pull on the other cabinet. A
2½-in. reveal in the corner is usually
sufficient to avoid problems. On wall
cabinets that meet at a 90° inside
corner, the adjacent doors don't usually need as much room as a base
corner doors; 1¾ in. is a good spacing.
With a 45° corner cabinet, the reveals
can be 1½ in.

As you decide on your reveals, don't
rely entirely on these guidelines.
Instead, visualize every new door and
drawer front as it will be opening up.
Think of them in relation to each other
and in terms of other objects, such as
nearby door and window casings, projecting soffit lights, and built-in
microwaves; then adjust the spacings
to accommodate any obstructions.
That's a much better way to work,
because you won't overlook any oddball situations. For example, if you are

converting from a partial-inset style to
a variable-overlay style (see the sidebar
on pp. 22-23), be aware when calculating drawer sizes that some
partial-overlay fronts project from the
face frames about ½ in. (see the drawing above), but when the new overlay
fronts are installed, they will project
the total thickness of the door (about
¾ in.), plus the added thickness of a
bumper pad (about ⅛ in.) and the
depth of the pull (which may or may
not be the same as the old pull). This
means some reveals (like the ones in
corners) may need to be bigger with
the new style door than they were
with the old.

Another situation to be aware of
when calculating spacings is on the
top rail of base cabinets. If the current
countertop has a drop edge, it probably overhangs the face frame ¾ in.
(see the drawing above). If you intend

Not many years ago, most kitchen cabinets were built in place. Such cabinets are usually well constructed and certainly worth refacing, but they do require a particular measuring approach to determine the width of new doors.

Unlike most modern cabinets, which are built and hung as individual boxes, each with its own face frame, built-in cabinets have one face frame for the entire run, and many of the doors share a common stile. For example, in the drawing at right, the hinge stiles of doors #2 and #3 are also the latch stiles of doors #1 and #4, respectively.

Because it's impossible to measure the width of individual cabinet face frames with built-in cabinetry, you have to divide the framework into imaginary cabinet sections relative to the door layout. In the bottom part of the drawing, the single face frame has been divided into five theoretical cabinet sections. A logical dividing point is often at the center of dividing stiles, and since doors #5 and #6 swing together, the frame is divided as if those two doors were on one cabinet.

Once the imaginary divisions are determined, you can then record the widths and use them to calculate new door widths, as described in the main text. Some stiles—for example, the hinge stiles of doors #2 and #3—may need to be widened with extension strips (see pp. 98-99) to accommodate the new door style and layout.

Modern cabinets vs. built-ins

This typical length of wall cabinetry shows door swings.

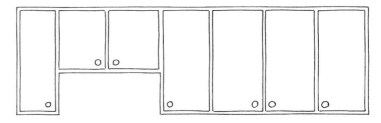

In a modern-style face frame, each cabinet is an individual framed unit.

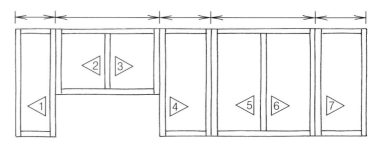

In a built-in face frame, the entire run of cabinets has only one frame.

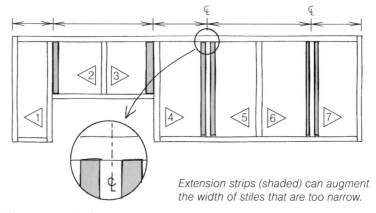

Extension strips (shaded) can augment the width of stiles that are too narrow.

When measuring for doors on built-in cabinets, you divide the cabinets into imaginary individual cabinets, usually by measuring to the center of shared stiles.

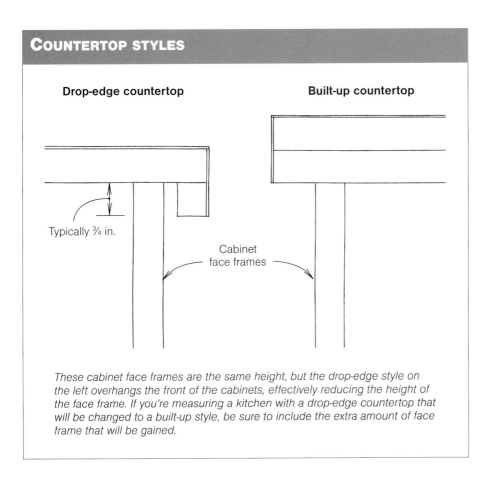

Drop-edge countertop

Built-up countertop

Typically ¾ in.

Cabinet
face frames

These cabinet face frames are the same height, but the drop-edge style on the left overhangs the front of the cabinets, effectively reducing the height of the face frame. If you're measuring a kitchen with a drop-edge countertop that will be changed to a built-up style, be sure to include the extra amount of face frame that will be gained.

to keep the same countertop or make a new one with the same drop-edge construction method, then figure your measurements to the bottom of the edge. However, if you plan to install a new countertop using the more modern built-up style, which rests on top of the cabinets without hanging down, then you'll need to take that into account and add the ¾ in. to your measurements.

MEASURING FOR FULL-OVERLAY STYLES

Refacing existing Euro-style frameless cabinetry with new full-overlay doors would probably be the easiest reface project you could ever want. The new doors would be exactly the same size

as the old doors—all you'd have to do is measure the old doors and switch the cup hinges from old to new. Thus far I haven't run into such a job, but it's bound to happen when the new frameless cabinets being installed these days start to show some age. For now though, most people who want to reface with full-overlay doors have face-frame cabinets to contend with.

If you opt for the full-overlay style in your kitchen (as I did in mine), keep in mind that the clearances between door and drawer fronts are actually nothing more than mini face-frame reveals. How small you make these reveals is determined by the type of cup hinge you use, the distance the

Top of doors:
¼ in. to ½ in.

Hinge to hinge:
½ in.

Hinge to latch:
½ in.

End of
cabinet:
¼ in.

Bottom of
cabinet:
¼ in. to ½ in.

Against
wall: ½ in.

Between double doors: ⅛ in.

Top of drawers: ½ in.

Between drawers:
¼ in. to ½ in.

Bottom of
cabinet:
¼ in. to ½ in.

Against wall: ½ in.
(see note below)

Note: If a base cabinet with a door hinged against the wall contains slide-out shelves, the reveal should be increased so the door (with pull) can open completely out of the way of the shelves.

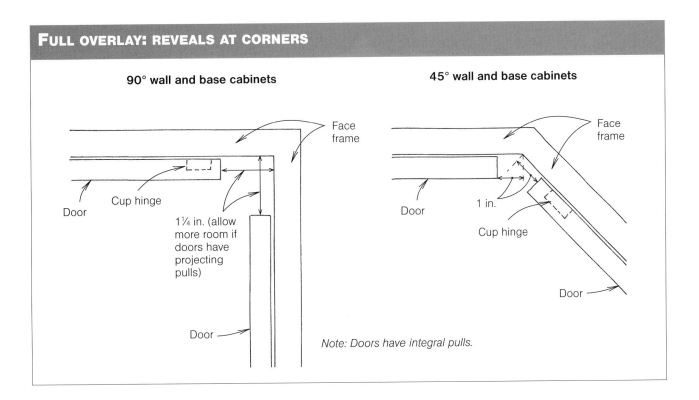

90° wall and base cabinets

Face frame

Cup hinge

Door

1¼ in. (allow more room if doors have projecting pulls)

Door

45° wall and base cabinets

Face frame

Door

1 in.

Cup hinge

Door

Note: Doors have integral pulls.

cup hole is drilled from the edge of the door, and the door thickness. That's a lot to take into account, but the information is readily available from the hinge manufacturer and is often shown in catalogs that sell the hinges (more about this on pp. 81-85).

If getting the absolute minimum spacings is not so critical to you, then I recommend the full-overlay reveals shown in the drawings on the facing page and above. Such spacings are usually more than adequate for any combination of door and cup hinge and leave a little space for fudging (see pp. 140-141). Nevertheless, if you decide to use these spacings, double-check your particular hinge specifications to make sure there won't be any problems.

If you are using a slab-type door with an integral flush pull (see p. 27) be aware that the lack of projecting knobs or pulls means that the reveal on base cabinet inside corners can be reduced from 2½ in. to 1¼ in.

With traditional overlay doors, minor measuring mistakes can usually be disguised by altering one or more reveals when the doors are installed. With full-overlay doors, discrepancies are harder to camouflage because the smaller reveals mean less room for fudging. However, if you happen to get in a situation where a laminate slab door is too big, it may be possible to rip one edge down on the table saw and reband it without too much trouble. That little trick once saved me from having to buy a whole new door.

The master drawing is used to record cabinet dimensions and derive door sizes. All the pertinent information is deliberately placed and conveniently referenced on one big sheet.

MAKING A MASTER DRAWING

As a first step to figuring the sizes of your new door and drawer fronts, draw a front view of your cabinets on paper. Because this will be your reference for, and record of, all measurements, I will call it the master drawing. On this drawing, all corners and angles in the plan will need to be "flattened" to create a continuous frontal diagram. To minimize the confusion that can result from drawings on several sheets of paper, it's a good idea to transfer all the cabinet information onto one piece of paper. You will probably have to tape sheets together in one long scroll.

The master drawing need not be to a particular scale, but it should at least be properly proportioned. It should also be neat and not too small. Obviously, the larger you draw your cabinets, the bigger the drawing will be and the easier it will be to read. If you're not adept at drawing, you'll find it helpful to use graph paper.

As you mark the locations for cabinets, include spaces for valances, stoves, and dishwashers. It's useful to know where these things are, and if you're a novice at calculating sizes from drawings, they will also help you find your way around what might otherwise be a confusing diagram.

Number the doors and drawers

When you have drawn in all the cabinets, number each door and drawer front. Start with the wall-cabinet door at the far left of your drawing and number all wall-cabinet doors in the kitchen plan in sequence, ending at the far right. Then return to the base-cabinet door on the left and continue number the base-cabinet doors, again proceeding from left to right. Numbering the cabinets in a layout is a standard measuring procedure used by kitchen designers. However, for refacing, you number the individual doors. Draw a circle around the door numbers to highlight them, and add triangle points so that one corner of the triangle aims at the hinge side of the door (door-swing information will come in handy at a later date).

Next, number the drawer fronts separately by assigning a new series of numbers, starting on the left and working to the right. To avoid confusion between door and drawer numbers, prefix the drawer fronts with the letters DF.

Measure your cabinets

Now you need to indicate measurements on your drawing in a deliberate and logical manner. Start by noting the most critical horizontal measurements; these are the overall length of each straight section of cabinet and the width of the individual cabinets that make up each straight run. If your kitchen is composed of individual cabinets, measuring the width of each will be a cinch, but if you have built-in cabinets, the measuring will be slightly more complicated (see the sidebar on p. 58). Measuring the individual width is critical because, as you'll shortly see, door measurements will be figured by starting with the total width of the

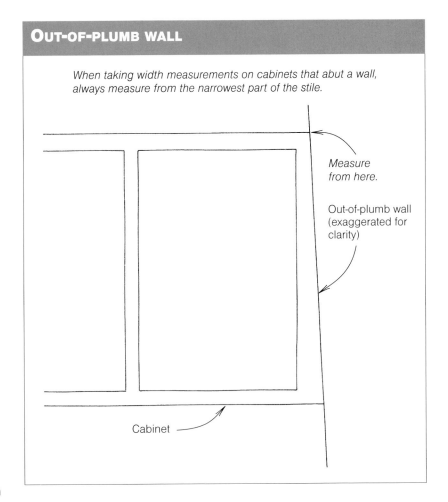

OUT-OF-PLUMB WALL

When taking width measurements on cabinets that abut a wall, always measure from the narrowest part of the stile.

Measure from here.

Out-of-plumb wall (exaggerated for clarity)

Cabinet

cabinet and subtracting the desired face-frame reveals from each side. Measuring the total length of straight runs serves as a double-check: Add up the individual cabinets and they should equal the total distance as measured. Take note when measuring whether the cabinet stiles that abut walls are tapered to conform to an out-of-plumb wall. When this is the case, take your width measurement from the narrowest point of the stile (see the drawing above).

Next, turn your attention to the vertical measurements in the plan. Start with the wall cabinets by measuring and noting the total height of each. Then do the same on the base cabinets, but

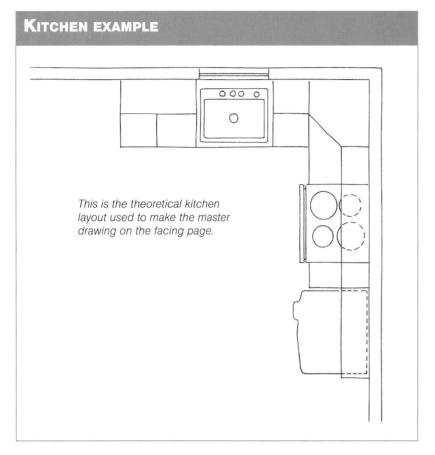

This is the theoretical kitchen layout used to make the master drawing on the facing page.

new kitchen. It might be a good idea to indicate what these will be somewhere on your main drawing.

The photo on p. 62 shows the master drawing I made for my own kitchen. But rather than use that to explain how to put together a master drawing and use it to calculate door sizes, we'll use the simpler L-shaped kitchen layout shown in the drawing at left instead. The master drawing that corresponds to this layout is shown in the drawing on the facing page. In the text that follows, the discussion refers to this master drawing.

DOING THE MATH

You are now about to perform a set of careful calculations that are absolutely critical to the success of your kitchen reface job. Pick a time and a place where you can work uninterrupted, and focus your full attention on the task at hand. Make your notations in a clear, organized, and deliberate manner on a measurement calculation sheet, as I'm about to explain. Don't do your figuring on a scrap of paper, jot the result down, and toss the "evidence" that you used to arrive at the verdict. Your measurement calculation sheet will act as a record and reference to all the measurements and materials needed for the job. Just as with the master drawing, it's prudent to tape several separate pages together into one easily referenced information log.

Because the calculation sheet shows clearly how each measurement is arrived at, you can easily double-check your calculations before ordering, and have a reference of how the door sizes with reveals should fit on the cabinets when it comes time to reface.

here you have drawers to contend with so you should draw a separate elevation "key" for each style of base cabinet (like the drawer base in the drawing on the facing page), and make sure to put it somewhere off to the side of your main drawing. Add the vertical measurements and compare them with the overall face-frame height measurement. Indicate all measurements clearly, then check and double-check them for accuracy.

Now your drawing is essentially done. But before you can determine your door and drawer-front sizes, you'll need to decide on the face-frame reveals you intend to aim for in your

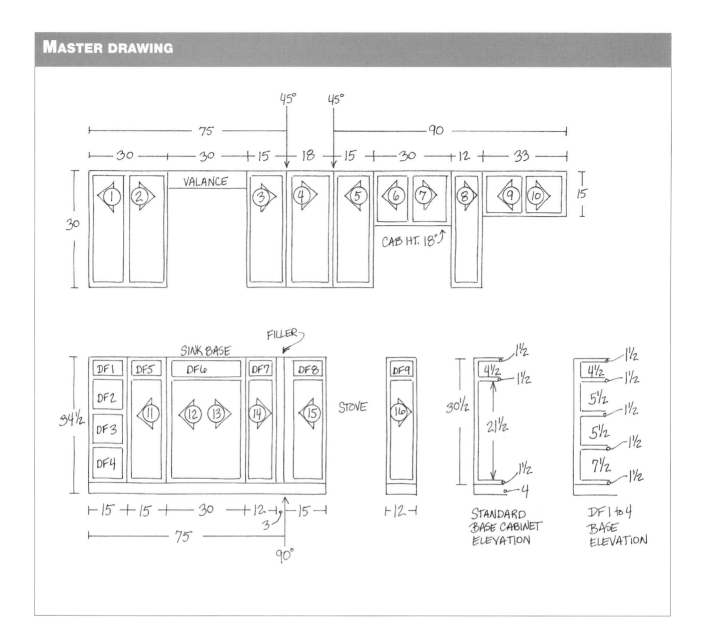

When I work, I use a simple shorthand with straightforward abbreviations (see the key to abbreviations on p 66). All measurements are in inches.

Figuring width

Figure the widths first. Start your calculations with door #1, and progress through the rest of the doors. This is done by taking the total width of the cabinet and then subtracting the left reveal and the right reveal. For example, for 1-in. reveals, the width of door #4 on the master drawing is figured as follows:

#4

$18CW - 1L - 1R = 16$ in. DW

For width calculations

CW = cabinet width
DW = door width
L = left reveal
R = right reveal
C = center reveal
LSP = left side panel
RSP = right side panel
F = filler

For height calculations

CH = cabinet height
DH = door height or drawer height
OH = opening height
T = top reveal
B = bottom reveal
M = molding
TF = total face-frame height
TR = total reveals

On a cabinet with two doors (#1 and #2 in the master drawing) that meet at a center stile with a $\frac{1}{2}$-in. center reveal, the individual door sizes are calculated as follows:

#1 and #2

$30CW - 1L - 1R - \frac{1}{2}C = 27\frac{1}{2}$

$27\frac{1}{2} \div 2 = 13\frac{3}{4}$ in. DW

Accounting for side panels When figuring widths of doors on cabinets that will be covered with side panels, keep in mind that the thickness of the side-panel material may affect cabinet widths, and thus door sizes. If cabinet sides will be skinned with veneer, whether by itself or phenolic backed (more about these materials in the next chapter), the added thickness is usually not enough to warrant any changes in width calculations. However, if you choose to use $\frac{1}{4}$-in. plywood panels, they are thick enough to make a difference. If the cabinet in the previous example had $\frac{1}{4}$-in. side panels, their width would be added to the cabinet width before the reveals were deducted. The width of the doors would be figured as follows:

#1 and #2

$30CW + \frac{1}{4}LSP + \frac{1}{4}RSP = 30\frac{1}{2}$

$30\frac{1}{2} - 1L - 1R - \frac{1}{2}C = 28$

$28 \div 2 = 14$ in. DW

However, when thicker side panels on a tall cabinet butt up under a shorter cabinet, the extra width that is added to the tall cabinet must then be subtracted from the short one. If you fail to do this calculation, the doors on the short cabinet will end up too wide—and the reveals will be too small. To illustrate what I mean, let's assume that in our example, $\frac{1}{4}$-in. side panels

are put on the cabinets that hold doors #5, #8, and #9/10, the width calculations for doors #5 through #10 would be as follows:

#5

$15CW + \frac{1}{4}RSP = 15\frac{1}{4}$

$15\frac{1}{4} - 1L - 1R = 13\frac{1}{4}$ in. DW

#6 and #7

$30CW - \frac{1}{4}LSP - \frac{1}{4}RSP = 29\frac{1}{2}$

$29\frac{1}{2} - 1L - 1R - \frac{1}{2}C = 27$

$27 \div 2 = 13\frac{1}{2}$ in. DW

#8

$12CW + \frac{1}{4}LSP + \frac{1}{4}RSP = 12\frac{1}{2}$

$12\frac{1}{2} - 1L - 1R = 10\frac{1}{2}$ in. DW

#9 and #10

$33CW - \frac{1}{4}LSP + \frac{1}{4}RSP = 33$

$33 - 1L - 1R - \frac{1}{2}C = 30\frac{1}{2}$

$30\frac{1}{2} \div 2 = 15\frac{1}{4}$ in. DW

The calculations we've done thus far have been simplified to show you how this sort of work is done. However, in many real kitchens (particularly built-in ones), the dimensions will not be so even. For example, if your two-door cabinet is an odd width and you choose a side reveal like $\frac{7}{8}$ in. (which I occasionally do), the calculation might go something like this:

$29\frac{15}{16}CW + \frac{1}{4}LSP = 30\frac{3}{16}$

$30\frac{3}{16} - \frac{7}{8}L - \frac{7}{8}R - \frac{3}{8}C = 28\frac{1}{16}$

$28\frac{1}{16} \div 2 = 14\frac{1}{32}$ in. DW

For most people, figuring complicated fractional calculations is not much fun, and mistakes are easy to make. The whole process can be simplified by using a tape measure and a scrap length of board to measure and figure on. With fronts, the smallest increment you need to deal with is sixteenths of an inch; door makers don't figure any closer than that and typically allow themselves a leeway of plus or minus $\frac{1}{16}$ in. So the $14\frac{1}{32}$-in. door width arrived at in the previous example can be rounded down to 14 in. or up to $14\frac{1}{16}$ in. Or one door could be 14 in. and the other $14\frac{1}{16}$ in. With traditional face-frames styles, minor discrepancies in reveals are not evident, and when the doors are installed, there are always small adjustments to be made. But at this stage, be as precise as you can with the calculations.

Accounting for fillers The width of the base-cabinet door and drawer fronts are figured the same as the top doors, but keep in mind the need for larger reveals at the corners (see pp. 56-57). In our kitchen example (see drawing on p. 64), the corner cabinets to the right of the sink hold doors #14 and #15. There is a 3-in. filler on the hinge side of door #14. I would figure the widths of these doors as follows:

#14

$$12CW + 3F = 15$$

$$15 - 1L - 2\frac{1}{4}R = 11\frac{3}{4} \text{ in. DW}$$

#15

$$15CW - 2\frac{1}{4}L - 1R = 11\frac{3}{4} \text{ in. DW}$$

Note that the corner filler is a factor only for door #14. Fillers are added between cabinets to fill spaces, and they may be located anywhere in the plan (top cabinets too). Fillers can range in size from a fraction of an inch up to 6 in. or more, though most are 3 in. or less. When sizing doors, you'll want to make fillers disappear visually by increasing door widths on one or both sides of the filler.

Sometimes, however, it isn't practical to expand door sizes to cover fillers. In the kitchen shown in the photo on p. 51, you can see two false panels on either side of the stove. When I cut the 40-in.-wide cabinet out to install the appliance, I had about 4 in. of useless space left on each side (too small for a door). I could have made the adjacent door and drawer fronts wider to cover the space, but I thought that would be a bit too much. The other alternative was to rebuild the cabinets on either side, but my client didn't go for that, so applied filler overlay panels take up the slack. They look much better than a wide expanse of open face frame.

Drawer fronts Drawer-front widths should correspond to the door widths below them. When figuring sink fronts or wide drawers over a double-door arrangement, be sure to add the space between doors into the front measurement. If it happens that you size a door to cover an excess of face frame and the drawer front above it ends up fitting off center on the drawer box (see the photo at bottom right on p. 149), don't worry. Things will look a little odd when the door is open, but perfect when the door is closed.

Figuring height

Figuring heights is usually simpler than figuring widths. Wall-cabinet door heights are figured by subtracting the top and bottom reveals from the cabinet height (refer to the drawing on p. 55 for suggested reveals). Show your math near the width calculations on the measurement calculation sheet. One example for each different cabinet height is sufficient. Here are the figures for a wall cabinet in the sample kitchen:

#1

$$30CH - \frac{1}{2}T - \frac{1}{2}B = 29 \text{ in. DH}$$

WALL CABINET WITH TOP MOLDING

Closed soffit	*Molding at the top of the cabinetry will affect face-frame dimensions and should be taken into account when figuring door heights and reveals.*
Cabinet	Molding

Face-frame height without molding

Face-frame height with molding

If the upper cabinets have an applied molding around their top, such as when they meet up to a closed soffit (see the drawing above), the molding will need to fit over and rest against part of the top of the face frames. You need to take this overlap into account in your calculations. I recommend that you commit ½ in. of solid wood at the top of the cabinets for this purpose. If your molding piece is quite narrow, the bearing surface will, of course, be narrower. If the sample kitchen had an applied molding that I planned to have

overlap the top of the wall cabinets by ½ in., the height for doors #1 and #2 would be calculated as follows:

#1 and #2

$$30CH - \tfrac{1}{2}T - \tfrac{1}{2}B - \tfrac{1}{2}M = 28\tfrac{1}{2} \text{ in. DH}$$

If you decide to cover the bottom of the wall cabinets with a ¼-in. bottom panel, you'll need to take that into account also, just as you did for side panels when calculating door widths (see the discussion on pp. 66-67).

Base-cabinet doors and drawers For figuring base-cabinet door and drawer heights, you'll refer to the separate base-cabinet elevations on your master diagram, but for the purpose of this discussion, refer to the drawing on the facing page. Here, we are aiming for reveals of ½ in. at the top, bottom, and middle (between the door and the drawer). Start with the drawer-opening height and add ½ in. to the bottom for overlap. (You can use ⅜ in. for overlays in a pinch, but try not to go any less.) Then to the height of the opening add whatever your elevation key measurements show is the amount that will leave ½ in. of top reveal. With the 1½-in.-wide top rail in our example, we'll need to add 1 in. to our front. So the calculation for the drawer height would be:

$$4\tfrac{1}{2} \text{ OH} + \tfrac{1}{2}B + \tfrac{1}{2}T = 5\tfrac{1}{2} \text{ in. DH}$$

To figure the height of the door below the drawer, subtract the drawer height and the three face-frame reveals from the total face-frame height, as follows:

$$30\tfrac{1}{2} \text{ TF} - 5\tfrac{1}{2} \text{ DH} - 1\tfrac{1}{2} \text{ TR} = 23\tfrac{1}{2} \text{ in. DH}$$

In our example, this door height will end up overlapping the middle rail ½ in., which is just right. However, if the rail were narrower, a door height of 23½ in. might not cover by ½ in. In fact, if the rail were only 1 in. wide, the door wouldn't overlap it at all. But that's perfectly okay, because you can add a strip of wood to the bottom of the rail before veneering. When it comes time to do the actual refacing, one of the first things you'll do is map out all these measurements on the face frames and add extension strips to rails and stiles as necessary to ensure that all doors and drawer fronts overhang the face frames by at least ⅜ in. to ½ in. Once the frames are veneered, nobody will ever know the difference.

On base cabinets with a single tall door and no drawers, the door height should equal the height of a top drawer, center reveal, and bottom door. The top drawer in a stack of drawers should be the same height as other top drawers, and the drawers below it should fall within the height range of adjoining single doors (see the drawing on p. 38) and with equal reveals between them all.

There you have it. You just waded through the fundamentals of measuring door and drawer fronts. Some kitchens are a piece of cake to figure, while others are a tough nut. Unusual situations will require some careful deliberation and possibly a little imagination to resolve, but if you approach the task in a logical way, taking into account each variable and foible of the layout, you will be able to put together the right sizes to do the job, and the best sizes to achieve a very pleasing custom look. The trouble is worth the effort.

BASE-CABINET DOOR AND DRAWER HEIGHTS

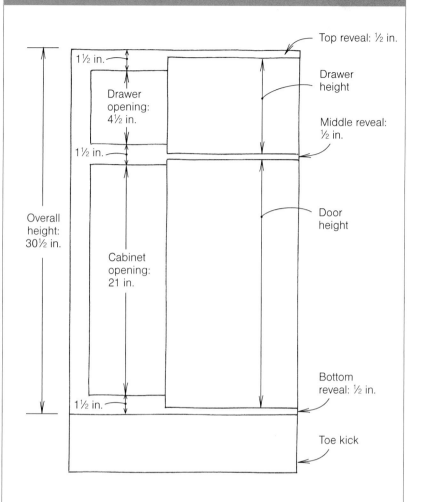

Calculating the height of a door with one drawer front over it is simple if you use your master-drawing elevation key, your predetermined face-frame reveals, and this three-step process. Figuring drawer bases will require a few more steps, but the idea is the same.

1. Subtract the top reveal (½ in.) from the top face-frame width (1½ in.) to get the top-drawer overlay (1 in.).

2. Add the top drawer overlay (1 in.) to the opening height (4½ in.) and the bottom drawer overlay (½ in.). The total (6 in.) is the drawer-front height.

3. Subtract the drawer height above (6 in.) and the top, middle, and bottom reveals (1½ in. total) from the total face-frame height (30½ in.) to get the door height (23 in.).

4

ORDERING MATERIALS

With your door and drawer-front sizes figured, it's time to line up the materials you'll need to do the refacing. There are plenty of choices to be made, and this chapter will give you the information you'll need to make the right decisions.

DOORS AND DRAWER FRONTS

When it comes to getting the door and drawer fronts you need, you have three choices: buying them, building them yourself, or having someone else build them for you. As with most things, each course of action has its pros and cons.

I'm a professional remodeler, but I've never made doors for any of my clients on a reface project. Although I have enough equipment to get the job done, my basic shop setup isn't well suited to producing doors on a regular basis. Besides, I can usually buy finished doors of any style for less than I could make them myself. Furthermore, it's just a whole lot easier to have other people make the doors for me—it's wear and tear on their machinery, sawdust and finish fumes in their lungs, and complete responsibility for a good product in their hands.

Be that as it may, from my perspective as a homeowner who was refacing his own kitchen cabinets (and didn't have to pay for labor), I decided to save money by making my own doors. To keep the cost down and streamline the construction process, I chose a frame-and-flat panel door style, which was very easy to put together. If you're an experienced woodworker or a zealous novice with the proper equipment and know-how to build and finish doors and you decide to make them yourself too, more power to you. If you need a little help, consult the cabinetmaking books listed in Further Reading on p. 159.

However, if you prefer to have someone else make the doors and fronts for you, you can either hire a small-scale local woodworker to make them or you can order from a large-scale supplier who specializes in making doors. The local woodworker may give you more personalized service, and it is usually nicer to deal with a local business. But chances are good that doors from a local cabinetmaker will be more expensive than doors from a larger-scale door maker. And, contrary to what you might think, local hand craftsmanship does not necessarily mean you'll get a better job. You might, but large-scale door suppliers usually do a very decent job. In fact, many local cabinetmakers make their own cabinets, but rarely their own doors—they buy them from a door manufacturer.

In Resources on pp. 155-157 I have listed several door suppliers that I'm aware of; there are, no doubt, many more throughout the country. I urge you to contact these people for information on their products. If you're fortunate enough to live near a door supplier, go check out the operation. That's what I did when I became interested in refacing.

Unfortunately, there are some suppliers who will deal only with professionals. If you're a nonprofessional, this book will give you the background knowledge you need to communicate intelligently with a supplier, but that may not make a difference. If you're a homeowner looking for doors, your choice of sources may be a little limited, but there are still plenty of suppliers who will gladly serve you. One way around this problem is to hire a reputable local professional to act as a buyer for you. Absolve this person of any responsibility for ordering mistakes (you measure and fill out the order) or the quality of the product (you check it out beforehand), and offer a modest but fair flat fee. Most pros would probably be delighted to make a few bucks for being the middleman and not doing any work.

Evaluating quality

Before you dish out the money for a kitchen full of doors, you need to make sure that the doors you'll be ordering are of high quality. I strongly recommend that you get a sample door from the manufacturer to be sure that you like the craftsmanship as well as the style and color you've chosen. Better yet, if you're in a position to look at a kitchen where the door-maker's product has been used, do it.

How do you recognize a well-made door? For plastic laminate or vinyl doors, differences in quality from one product to another are likely to be minor. If the door looks good and comes from an established manufacturer with a guarantee that covers warpage, it's probably as good as the next. However, with wood doors, there are definitely variations in quality. Most of the distinctions are visual, but you need to know what you're looking for.

First, there is the matter of the quality of wood used. As mentioned on p. 10, many door suppliers offer a choice of different grades of wood. The additional cost for the better grades is usually money well spent. However, a good grade alone is no guarantee of a good-looking door. Even Select lumber has variations in grain color and pattern. The center panels in solid-panel doors are a key indication of quality. They consist of glued-together pieces of wood, and in better-quality doors, the center panel appears to be a single wide piece of wood because there is little or no clear distinction between the pieces. The grain patterns between boards flow into each other; there is no exaggerated grain against straight grain. Better doors have boards no narrower than 3 in. to 4 in. with the grain matched, while lesser-quality doors have panels that consist of more pieces of smaller sizes and little or no grain matching.

Sanding is an important part of the door-manufacturing process, and on better-quality doors, milling marks and minor burns from shaper blades are hand-sanded away. When assembled, frame-and-panel doors are run through wide-belt sanding machines and sanded parallel with the grain of the panel; this leaves minor cross-grain sanding marks on the top and bottom rails. On better-quality doors, these marks are sanded away. Cross-grain sanding marks are also removed from the back of better-quality doors, although the appearance of the back of the door is not such a critical factor. Well-made doors have no visible glue residue, and the joints where rails and stiles meet will be tight.

Finished vs. unfinished doors You can buy doors that are finished or unfinished. On finished doors, the surface should be smooth and even, without runs. Less obvious but equally important is the kind of top coat (after any stains and sealers go on) that was applied. Opinion differs on what finish is best for kitchen doors. A catalyzed lacquer or conversion varnish is commonly used, and either of these forms a hard and durable film. Steer away from doors finished with noncatalyzed "old-fashioned lacquer." Lacquer may be great on fine furniture, but the finish is too soft for kitchen cabinets. Also, lacquer requires periodic waxing; the other finishes don't.

If you buy unfinished doors, you will have to finish them yourself. I spray-finished the doors in my own kitchen with three coats of a clear water-based finish (similar to polyurethane) that I applied with a high-volume, low-pressure (HVLP) sprayer. If I had hand-finished the fronts I would have used a wipe-on oil-based finish because it's a simple finish to apply. In any event, if you plan to finish your own doors, see Further Reading on p. 159 for some good books on the subject.

Reading the product literature

Rule number one when ordering door and drawer fronts is to read the door maker's product literature carefully and follow the ordering instructions to the letter. My own experience in ordering doors is pretty much limited to one supplier. I have been so pleased with that company's product and services that I've never seriously considered ordering from anyone else. My supplier is only about an hour's drive away, and that's a plus in my book too. Of course, there are plenty of other good door suppliers. I've seen some of their products at national woodworking shows, I have collected their sales literature, and I have even ordered some of the sample doors shown elsewhere in this book from them.

If there is one thing I've learned from all the literature I've assembled, it is that everyone does things a little bit differently. Some have colorful sales literature, some don't. Some sell prefinished veneer, plywood, moldings, and even hardware, and some don't. One supplier sells only unfinished doors. Another supplier won't drill the back of doors for cup hinges. And they all seem to have a slightly different approach to figuring a door's price.

Despite the differences, though, there are a couple of considerations that you should be aware of when ordering from any supplier. To start, each supplier has minimum sizes for different door styles. For example, the minimum width that my supplier will make a square raised-panel door is 7½ in., and the narrowest cathedral raised panel is 8¼ in. But if the width of the door-frame pieces is reduced (from 2¼ in. to 2 in.), I can get those minimum dimensions down to 7 in. and 7¾ in., respectively. If I need a narrower raised-panel door than that, I have to get a drawer front with a raised profile and hinge it like a door. That solution works out relatively well, but an even better solution is to modify something (a reveal maybe) to gain enough room for a whole frame-and-panel door.

All manufacturers set maximum limits on single-panel door sizes that they'll guarantee (the major concern is warpage). Tall frame-and-panel doors, as for a pantry cabinet, or tall wall cabinets, may require two panels, one over the other. My supplier specifies that doors over 44 in. high must have two panels to qualify for his warpage guarantee. In addition, he won't guarantee doors more than 24 in. wide, again for warpage reasons.

One final bit of advice on the subject of ordering doors (or whatever else you need) is to use the manufacturer's order form, fill it out clearly, and keep a copy. If problems regarding specifications arise, the order form usually settles the matter of who's to blame. And if you need to attach an extra page of drawings or instructions, it's always a good idea to refer to it on the main order form. If you write "see attached pages for further details

Flexible wood veneer with a pressure-sensitive adhesive backing is the most common type of veneer used for refacing cabinets.

about moldings," it's not nearly as likely that those moldings will be overlooked or made incorrectly.

WOOD VENEER

Wood veneer is a thin sheet of wood—real wood. More than once, I've had clients who were skeptical that the prefinished veneer sample I showed them was genuine wood and not plastic. The most common question regarding veneer is related to durability. My answer is always the same: Veneer is as durable as whatever it's applied over. If the veneer is put on a piece of foam, you can poke a hole through it with relative ease, but if it's applied to a solid-wood material, it's as durable as the underlayment. Likewise, the finish is as durable on veneer as it would be on anything else.

As for how well the veneer sticks and whether or not it will stay stuck, if it is applied properly (I'll show you how in Chapter 6) the material sticks incredibly well and stays that way. The simple fact of the matter is that some of the world's finest furniture is veneered, so why not kitchen cabinets?

Having made my case for veneer, let me quickly add a couple of little caveats. Excessive moisture or heat may compromise the bond. If, for example, the plumbing under the sink springs a leak, runs out the front of the cabinet, and saturates the veneered bottom rail, wood veneer won't fare as well as solid wood. And, although I've never seen it happen, in theory, excessive amounts of steam from a cooktop could lead to delamination. Extreme heat from ovens or stoves could also lead to problems, although I've never seen this happen either. I would be concerned about it only if the existing cabinets indicated that there was a heat problem to begin with. In that case, I would find some way to mitigate the heat buildup before refacing.

Despite these minor drawbacks, veneer does have a redeeming quality—if it is damaged it can be removed (it's not easy but it can be done; see p. 123 for details). A damaged piece of veneer is less troublesome to replace than a damaged section of solid-wood face frame.

Veneer traditionally comes in slices of raw wood of random width and length that you must skillfully match up, cut

and join together, and then glue down. The veneer used in refacing, however, is preassembled into sheets of uniform size. The thin wood layer (about $\frac{1}{40}$ in. thick) is bonded to a paper backing. These sheets, usually referred to as flexible veneers, come either with a plain back—to which you apply the appropriate adhesive—or with a preglued back. Plain-backed flexible veneers can be used for refacing but I think preglued veneers are the only way to go.

Preglued veneers are available with a pressure-sensitive-adhesive backing or an iron-on, hot-melt adhesive backing. Pressure-sensitive veneer (also known as "peel-and-stick" veneer) is the kind commonly used in refacing, and it's the kind I recommend you use. Peeling away a protective cover sheet on the back exposes a sticky glue layer. Press the veneer in place, apply smoothing pressure, and the bond is permanent—no mess, no fuss. There is a bit more to know about getting the best possible bond, but that will be covered later (see pp. 113-115). For now, the point is that peel-and-stick veneers are easy to work with.

On veneer with a hot-melt adhesive backing, the glue is dry to the touch. Sheets of the material are applied by holding them in position while moving a regular household iron over the top surface. The heat activates the glue. The one advantage to iron-on veneer is that it's easier to position the sheets for glue-down. Peel-and-stick veneers are admittedly a little tricky to lay down because of the touch-and-grab nature of the adhesive. However, iron-on veneer can be more time-consuming to apply, and since the iron would essentially melt any pre-applied finish, the veneer must be installed unfinished, and then finished in place on the cabinets. This is all feasible, and there are still a few refacers who take this approach, but most professionals these days use pressure-sensitive veneers.

If the idea of using iron-on veneer appeals to you, then by all means do it. Much of the how-to information presented in the next chapter applies equally to hot-melt veneers, but from here on, when I speak of veneer, I'm referring to peel-and-stick. For specific differences in application between hot-melt and pressure-sensitive adhesives, consult the veneer manufacturer's application instructions.

Pressure-sensitive flexible veneer is readily available from many door suppliers, who will finish it to match your doors. The standard size is 2 ft. by 8 ft., although 4 ft. by 8 ft. is also available. If you are doing your own finishing, you can probably buy the sheets at your local lumberyard or home center. Chances are that these places won't stock the material, but can order it easily enough. Veneer is also available from many woodworking tool and material mail-order catalogs, a few of which I've listed in Resources on pp. 155-157.

If you opt to buy prefinished doors and unfinished veneer that you want to finish to match the doors, I recommend that you ask the door manufacturer what finish products were used on the doors and how to best make the match. Then experiment with the finish on some sample pieces of veneer to ensure the best possible finishing job. One refacer I know made the mistake of applying a water-based top-coat finish to the veneer when the doors were finished with a precatalyzed lacquer.

The color contrast was so unacceptable that he had to remove all the veneer and redo the whole job.

If you are buying flexible veneers for face frames, make sure to get 10-mil veneer. Thinner veneers are too flimsy for a high-quality job, and thicker veneers are not sufficiently flexible for bending around face frames. Veneer with 3M adhesive backing is the most widely used, and it's what I prefer.

Figuring face-frame veneer needs

If you'll be using 2-ft. by 8-ft. veneer sheets, if the kitchen does not have extra-large doors, and if the individual cabinet face frames are not more than 2 in. wide, you should be able to order one sheet of veneer for every 10 door and drawer openings, and have enough to do the job with less than a full sheet left over. For example, the sample kitchen layout in Chapter 3 (see the master drawing on p. 65) has a total of 25 openings. Divide that number by 10 and you end up with 2.5 sheets. Round the number up and get 3 full sheets. This method of calculating veneer should provide you with enough even if you waste a little veneer in the learning process.

PANEL MATERIALS

The same 10-mil flexible veneer that's used for covering face frames can theoretically be used it to cover areas like cabinet side panels and the back side of peninsula or island cabinets, but it usually isn't. The side pieces are much larger than the strips used on fronts, and such pieces can be unwieldy to lay in place. Also, minor cabinet irregularities will telegraph through the thin veneer if the underlying surface is not carefully prepared.

To skin cabinet sides, bottoms, toe kicks, peninsula back sides, and other flat areas that need to be resurfaced, ¼-in. plywood with a top-quality hardwood face veneer is the best choice.

with construction adhesive and countersunk small-head brads; the nail holes are then filled with colored putty. Construction adhesive doesn't stick on contact, so the panels can be easily positioned before they are tacked down. If you opt to cover the underside of wall cabinets, ¼-in. plywood is ideal because it's rigid enough to span the recessed bottoms on most cabinets. It's also well suited to covering the back side of island and peninsula cabinets, as well as toe kicks, refrigerator side panels, and the flat bottom of a soffit behind the sink valance.

For these reasons, other coverings are used. These include plywood, phenolic veneer, and three-ply veneer.

Plywood

Most refacers use ¼-in. hardwood-faced plywood (in the same species of wood as the new doors) for covering cabinet side panels and other large flat surfaces. The sheets cut easily with basic woodworking tools—some refacers even cut their ¼-in. plywood to rough size with a sharp utility knife. It is possible to get ⅛-in. sheets of plywood for panel skins, and some refacers prefer it because it's even easier to cut to size. I don't recommend it. If you're going to use plywood, steer clear of anything thinner than a nominal ¼ in. In my experience, ⅛-in. material doesn't lay on as flat and smooth as ¼-in. plywood.

With ¼-in. plywood, minor cabinet-side damage or loose paint can simply be covered over without the need for painstaking surface preparation. The plywood is cut to size and fastened on

Just as with all other reface materials, plywood can and should be prefinished prior to application—preferably using the same materials and techniques used to finish the doors and veneer.

You can usually buy 4x8 prefinished sheets of plywood from your reface supplier, and you can cut the pieces you need out of them. For a bit more money, some suppliers will cut plywood to your required dimensions. Precut pieces will be easier for you to manage, and the reduced sizes mean they can usually be shipped via common carrier, whereas full sheets of plywood are more complicated and costly to ship. (Shipping considerations are a concern only if you deal with a nonlocal material supplier.)

If you'll be doing your own finishing and want to line up a local source of unfinished plywood, you may want to do a little checking around to find the best material because quality can vary a lot. Grading is somewhat difficult to understand because suppliers may use different grading standards, but if you

Phenolic veneer is wood veneer bonded to a plastic-laminate backing (shown here on the bottom piece). Phenolic veneer is thinner than plywood, and it has no edge plies that would be visible from the underside of wall cabinets if used to cover their sides.

just make it clear that you want one good face with even color throughout and a respectable grain pattern, the supplier should be able to take it from there.

Big home centers may have the cheapest plywood around but not necessarily the good grades you want. If you don't know of a plywood-savvy lumberyard salesperson who can help you, I recommend that you call a large (probably wholesale) plywood distributor (check the Yellow Pages) and ask for assistance. You'll know a good plywood face when you see it. Don't settle for less than the best (unless you bought doors made with low-grade lumber) because the side panels, particularly on wall cabinets, are clearly visible. And using a better grade of ¼-in. plywood won't cost you a whole lot more.

Plywood with a composition (i.e., particleboard) wood core is becoming more popular. It's not as strong as traditional veneer-core plywood, but structural strength isn't really a concern here, so the composition product is probably fine. I've never used it, but I understand it works well and actually cuts more easily.

Phenolic veneer

Phenolic veneer is wood veneer that has been bonded to a sheet of plastic laminate. The total thickness of the sheet is just under ¹⁄₁₆ in., and the standard sheet size is 4 ft. by 8 ft. (reface suppliers will sell smaller sizes, too). Like the decorative plastic laminate used to make countertops, phenolic veneer sheets have some flexibility to them, so bigger sizes can be loosely rolled, boxed, and shipped by common carrier. However, phenolic veneer is not so flexible that you can wrap a face frame with it.

I use phenolic veneer quite often to cover the sides of wall cabinets because I don't like the look of exposed ¼-in. plywood end grain that shows underneath the cabinets (see

PLYWOOD SIDES ON A WALL CABINET

Bottom view

The edge of a side panel will show on the bottom of the cabinet. This is usually not a problem because cabinet bottoms are mostly out of sight. If you do find this objectionable, cover it with phenolic or three-ply veneer.

Front edge of side panel will be covered with veneer.

Face frame

¼-in. plywood side panel

Cabinet bottom

Plywood end grain will be visible from underneath.

Three-ply veneer

Three-ply veneer has three wood plies and no paper back. It's stiffer than flexible veneer but more flexible than phenolic. The veneer goes on like phenolic (using a contact cement). However, the thin wood can be cut and finished off more easily than phenolic or ¼-in. plywood. This veneer is relatively new to me. The first time I used it was on my own kitchen, but I expect to use it more often in place of phenolic veneer because it's easier to work with.

Calculating materials

You can use either one panel material exclusively or a combination of materials to cover whatever flat expanses need to be refaced. Figuring how much you need is a straightforward procedure; measure the areas and add an inch or two each way to give some extra material for scribing and fitting.

Plywood If you're dealing with a supplier who will cut skinning materials to size, order those sizes. When you order panel pieces, indicate the width first and then the length, with the length measurement running parallel to the grain of the wood. To make sure you get what you want, indicate clearly which dimension is the grain dimension of the sheet, perhaps with the notation GD after the number.

If you're figuring on using full sheets of materials, the calculating may require a tad more or less mental effort, depending on how close you want to figure it. There are no simple tricks to use here, although it might help to draw out on graph paper a scale diagram of a full sheet (4x8 or 2x8) and figure the arrangement of pieces on that. In any event, I urge you

the drawing above). (End grain toward the front of the cabinet is covered when the face frames are veneered.) How the bottoms of the cabinets look is not usually considered a major issue (except, perhaps, on high cabinets like the one over the refrigerator), but I still like them to look as good as possible.

The hard phenolic backing prevents minor surface imperfections in the cabinet underlayment from showing through. Phenolic veneer is a mite stiffer than flexible veneer, so the pieces are somewhat more manageable when putting them on.

If you're familiar with the methods used to fabricate with plastic laminate (see Chapter 7), you'll have no trouble working with phenolic veneer, which is also glued with contact cement and trimmed to size with a flush-trimming bit in a router.

Strip laminating
Individual pieces of oversize laminate strips are glued on and trimmed flush with the opening. This technique is commonly used with wood-grain-patterned laminates.

Sheet laminating
A full sheet of laminate is glued over wide sections of the face frame, and the openings are routed away. This technique works best with solid-color laminates.

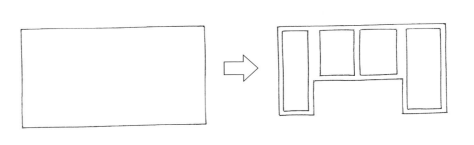

to assign an identification number to each panel piece on your master drawing, and then indicate the appropriate sizes on the master calculation sheet where you've figured door sizes. This information is essential for ordering materials and figuring out what goes where when you do the actual work.

Plastic laminate When refacing cabinets with plastic-laminate doors (see pp. 20-21 and p. 24), you'll want to use matching laminate to cover the sides and face frames. There are two approaches: strip laminating and sheet laminating (see the drawing above), and the method you use will affect the quantity and the type of laminate you use. In strip laminating, you cut strips of laminate and apply individual pieces to the face-frame rails and stiles. In sheet laminating, you glue large sheets of laminate over entire lengths of cabinet face frames and then trim out the door openings with a router.

Strip laminating is better if you are using laminate with a directional pattern, such as wood grain. Gluing on individual strips is also an option with solid colors, like white or almond, but sheet laminating makes for a faster job and a smooth, seam-free cabinet front. There is, however, considerable cutout waste with sheet laminating.

When strip-laminating face frames, you'll want to use vertical-grade laminate because it is thin and easily worked, and it's also less expensive. Typically, vertical-grade laminate comes only in 4x8 sheets. For sheet laminating, vertical grade will also do the job, but the limited sheet size will not cover long expanses of face frame in one piece. So another possibility is to use horizontal-grade laminate, which is the grade commonly used when making square-edged countertops. Horizontal grade is thicker (which means it will reveal a wider black line on the edges) and costs a bit more, but many sheet sizes are usually available—in widths of 24 in., 30 in., 36 in., 48 in., and 60 in., and in lengths of 8 ft, 10 ft., and 12 ft. Plastic laminate can be ordered from any home center or from your door supplier.

Rigid thermal foil RTF doors, as you'll recall from pp. 24-25, are made by heat-forming a sheet of vinyl plastic over a machine-shaped MDF door blank. Door manufacturers can supply you with the same vinyl material for strip-laminating cabinet face frames. However, many, if not most, RTF doors are sold in a basic white color, and some refacers will use a close match of white plastic laminate for covering face frames and skinning cabinet sides and backs. The laminate is easier to get, thicker, and more durable.

You can't bend vinyl or laminate around the inside of face frames, so to get the best finished look, you'll have to paint the inside edges of the rails and stiles (see p. 137). Get a quart of top-quality (usually the most expensive) latex paint from your local paint store, and have it custom-mixed to match your vinyl or plastic laminate.

HINGES

The door hinges you choose are a definite style consideration (see p. 28). Cup hinges, which are not visible when the doors are closed, are the only hinges suited for full-overlay cabinet doors, and they are also an option with traditional-style fronts. The

other option with traditional-style fronts is to use what's generally known (appropriately enough) as a traditional cabinet hinge. When refacing with traditional hinges, it is best to use a variable-overlay style.

Traditional cabinet hinges

Traditional-overlay hinges attach directly to the back of the door with three screws and to the cabinet face frame with two more screws. If a kitchen is only a few years old and the doors already have variable-overlay hinges, there is no reason why you can't reuse the same hinges, but in most instances it's probably best to get new ones.

For the most part, you can't tell much about the quality of traditional hinges by looking at them. Amerock is a well-known name in cabinet hardware, and I recommend any of their traditional cabinet hinges because I've used them and I'm a satisfied customer. The company has a decent warranty, which includes the finish. You'll find traditional cabinet hinges in virtually any building supply store, as well as some of the mail-order material catalogs I've listed in Resources on pp. 155-157.

How many hinges a door will need depends on its height and weight. Two is obviously the minimum, and two will be sufficient for most doors. On cabinet doors that are 36 in. or more in height, I'd advise adding a third hinge, and four hinges on a tall pantry door isn't too many. If you buy them by the full box (usually 25) they're cheaper than when purchased individually. Traditional hinges are available in self-closing or free-swinging types, and I recommend using the self-closing kind.

Cup hinges

Concealed cup hinges are so radically different from traditional-overlay hinges that they can be confusing to those not in the know. (Even I get confused sometimes, and I'm familiar with them.) There are so many types of cup hinge on the market—one catalog boasts more than 185 variations to choose from— that it is difficult to talk about cup hinges in general terms. For that reason this discussion will focus on one particular cup hinge. It's the cup hinge I use exclusively in my refacing work.

The Blum Compact 33 series, 110°-opening cup hinge is designed specifically for face-frame cabinetry. The cup part of the hinge fits into a 35mm-dia. hole drilled into the back of the door stile. Blum is a European company, so the specifications are in millimeters. If your brain is geared for inches, see the conversion chart at right.

You can usually have cup holes drilled by your door supplier for a couple of dollars more per door, or you can drill them yourself with a drill press and a 35mm drill bit. Although 35mm is pretty darn close to 1¼ in., don't use a 1¼-in. bit; get the right bit for the job. Cup-hinge drill bits are usually available from the sources that supply the hinges. And the drill press (preferably with some sort of homemade jig for holding the door in proper position) is pretty much a necessity because drilling by hand with an electric drill is difficult and unreliable. For professional-scale production work, Blum makes a special hinge-drilling and insertion machine.

METRIC EQUIVALENTS

Inches	Millimeters	
	Exact	Approximate
1/32	.79	1
1/16	1.59	1.5
3/32	2.38	2.5
1/8	3.18	3
5/32	3.97	4
3/16	4.76	5
7/32	5.56	5.5
1/4	6.35	6.5
9/32	7.14	7
5/16	7.94	8
11/32	8.73	9
3/8	9.53	9.5
13/32	10.31	10
7/16	11.11	11
15/32	11.90	12
1/2	12.70	12.5
17/32	13.49	13.5
9/16	14.29	14
19/32	15.08	15
5/8	15.88	16
21/32	16.67	16.5
11/16	17.46	17.5
23/32	18.26	18.5
3/4	19.05	19
25/32	19.84	20
13/16	20.64	20.5
27/32	21.43	21
7/8	22.23	23
15/16	23.81	24
31/32	24.60	24.5
1	25.40	25.5

Cup hinges come in screw-in and press-in versions. The screw-in type (right) can be used with solid wood doors. The press-in type (left) has plastic "dowels" that fit into predrilled 8mm holes. Dowels hold the screws and are necessary when attaching hinges to doors made of wood composites like MDF.

Hinge cups fit into the drilled cup hole and fasten on with two screws. On a solid-wood door, you can fasten the cup on by driving the appropriate screws (#7 by ⅝ in.—usually supplied with the hinge) directly into the wood. However if your doors are laminate slabs or RTF, the composition wood core of the door (MDF) is not considered strong enough material for holding the screws. A special plastic insert (referred to as a dowel by the manufacturer) is pressed into 8mm holes where the screws go. Screws then go into the dowels. All brands of hinge cups are available in a screw-in or press-in version (see the photo at left). The press-in version comes with screws and dowels attached.

If you have a door supplier drill your cup holes, make sure that the drilling will match the brand of hinge you'll be using. If you're drilling your own doors for press-in cups, use the drill press and place the holes very carefully.

How many cup hinges a door will need depends on its size and weight. Blum recommends the size/weight hinge guidelines shown in the chart at left; other manufactures have similar recommendations. For the typical door, two hinges is standard. The cup holes should be drilled so the edge of the hole is 2mm to 3mm from the edge of the door and about ½ in. deep. Space the center of the holes about 3½ in. from the top and bottom of the door.

Inside the hinge cup is a spring-loaded hinge arm that pivots in and out; the arm is out when the door is in the open position. To connect the door to a cabinet, the hinge arm is fastened to a mounting plate that is attached to the edge of the cabinet face frame.

BLUM HINGES NEEDED PER DOOR

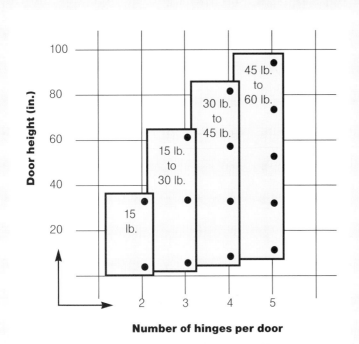

Door height (in.)

- 15 lb. (2 hinges)
- 15 lb. to 30 lb. (3 hinges)
- 30 lb. to 45 lb. (4 hinges)
- 45 lb. to 60 lb. (5 hinges)

Number of hinges per door

Courtesy Julius Blum Inc.

There are nine different mounting plates to choose from (see the chart at right). Mounting plates are bought individually, separate from the hinge cups, which are also purchased separately—unlike traditional hinges, which come in pairs.

When refacing a traditional face-frame cabinet with cup hinges, you will want to indicate the width of the cabinet hinge stiles on the master drawing (see p. 65). Then you need only to consult the drawing and the measurement calculation sheet to figure what mounting plates you'll need for each door. Just subtract the reveal from the width of the stile to get the door overlay.

The door swings indicated on the master drawing are important when using cup hinges because you have to make sure the cup holes and hinges are attached to the correct door edge. Although this isn't necessary with square raised-panel or slab doors (because the door can be turned to get right or left hinging), slabs with CWPs or panel shapes other than square must be drilled on the proper side. If your door supplier will be drilling for cup hinges, you'll want to indicate the hinge side on the order form.

Once you know the door overlay, you can order the appropriate mounting plates (see the chart at right). You'll note in the chart that the mounting-plate overlays only cover certain increments from $\frac{1}{4}$ in. up to $1\frac{3}{8}$ in. That's because the arm-to-plate attachment allows for adjustment from the stated amount down to $\frac{1}{8}$ in. less. Thus, a $\frac{9}{16}$-in. overlay can be achieved with a $\frac{5}{8}$-in. mounting plate. Why Blum broke the pattern of overlay increments by not offering a

MOUNTING PLATES FOR BLUM COMPACT 33 CUP HINGES

Mounting plate	Stated overlay (in.)	Overlay range (in.)
#130.110 24	$\frac{1}{4}$	$\frac{1}{8}$ to $\frac{1}{4}$
#130/110 23	$\frac{1}{2}$	$\frac{3}{8}$ to $\frac{1}{2}$
#130.110 26	$\frac{5}{8}$	$\frac{1}{2}$ to $\frac{5}{8}$
#130.110 22	$\frac{3}{4}$	$\frac{5}{8}$ to $\frac{3}{4}$
#130.111	1	$\frac{7}{8}$ to 1
#130.112	$1\frac{1}{8}$	1 to $1\frac{1}{8}$
#130.113	$1\frac{1}{4}$	$1\frac{1}{8}$ to $1\frac{1}{4}$
#130.114	$1\frac{3}{8}$	$1\frac{1}{4}$ to $1\frac{3}{8}$
#113.024	variable	$1\frac{3}{8}$ +

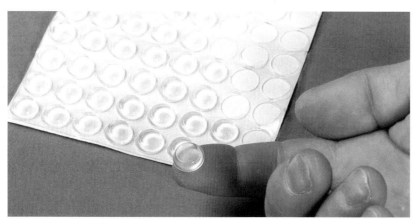

Self-stick clear-plastic bumper pads protect the cabinets from slamming doors and drawers.

⅜-in. mounting plate, I don't know. That omission leaves a ⅛-in. span from ¼ in. to ⅜ in. that you'll have to fudge somehow if you need it, but since you're aiming for a minimum ⅜-in. overlay on all doors, the missing plate shouldn't be any problem. For accommodating overlays that are greater than 1⅜ in., the flat face mounting plate (#113.024) will do the job. (Other plates mount to the side of the frame.)

The sideways, or overlay, adjustment is one adjustment feature of the Compact 33 hinge; another is up-and-down door adjustment, which is made possible by elongated plate-mounting holes. Unfortunately, there is no in-and-out adjustment, which would help correct the uneven closing of a door that's slightly warped or a cabinet that's slightly racked. Euro-style cup hinges that are used on frameless cabinetry do have this adjustment capability and it's a nice feature, but we refacers have to deal with such shortcomings by coming up with our own imaginative ways to solve in-and-out adjustments (see p. 141).

My biggest gripe with the Compact 33 hinges is that the overlay amount is not clearly marked on the plates and, except for the flat face mounting plate, it isn't immediately evident what the overlay is. The plates do have their model numbers stamped on them but there is no apparent relation between the model number and the plate size. If you use Blum face-frame hinges and get confused with the overlay plates, you can always attach one to a door and measure the overlay, or you can compare the code numbers to those on the chart on p. 83. I keep a supply of various mounting plates separated into plastic zipper-closing bags, with the overlays clearly marked on the outside.

You won't find cup hinges in every home center. Your best bet is to order them from a mail-order supplier who stocks the full selection of mounting plates (see Resources on pp. 155-157).

The adjusting screws on Blum cup hinges have what's called a #2 Pozi head on them, which is essentially a metric version of the common Phillips head. A #2 Phillips screwdriver will work for tightening them, buth the Pozi screwdriver grips much better.

Bumper pads

Regardless of the type of hinge you use, you're going to need bumper pads to cushion the doors and drawers as they close. Bumper pads can be made of cork, felt, foam rubber, or clear vinyl plastic. Some traditional hinges come with tiny, thin, self-stick cork or felt bumpers that will do the job—but not very well. I throw them out and use ⅛-in.-thick clear-plastic door bumpers (see the photo above left). I prefer this size and style because

I think they are better quality. Some-times I can hide a slight door warp by sanding a little off the thickness of one pad (see pp. 140-141). Two bumpers per door or drawer front are standard, and they are available from most hinge suppliers.

DRAWERS

If your old drawers are shot, you'll need new ones. You'll also need new drawers if you make new cabinets or certain modifications to your old cabi-nets. One refacer I know installs new drawers and slides with every reface job he does. He reasons that the refacing will last at least 25 years and to make sure the drawers hold together for that long, they should be replaced. I like his attitude, but I think that most old drawers, if they're still sound, can continue to serve well. Nevertheless, "fresh" clean new drawers are a very nice upgrade, and I offer it to my customers as an option.

If your job requires new drawers, you can either make them yourself or buy them custom made to your specifica-tions. The cabinetmaking books listed in Further Reading on p. 159 describe different methods for making drawers. Most reface-door suppliers also offer custom-sized drawers (see the photo above right), and there are companies that specialize in custom drawers.

Drawers are available as fully assem-bled units or as precut knock-down "kits." Drawer sides can be made of melamine or vinyl-coated MDF, ply-wood, or solid wood in various hardwood species. Wood sides can be prefinished or left natural for you to finish. Side thicknesses are ½ in., ⅝ in., or ¾ in. Drawer bottoms can be ⅛ in.

or ¼ in. thick, and they can be made of traditional wood plywood or com-position wood plywood. (I recommend the traditional ¼-in. plywood because it's stronger.) Bottoms can be natural wood or have a white or wood-grain surface of vinyl or melamine (the most durable).

Drawer bottoms typically fit into grooves milled into the drawer side pieces. From there, construction meth-ods for assembling the drawer sides to each other vary considerably. Sides can be doweled, rabbeted, or dovetailed (to name a few methods). Dovetails are revered as the pinnacle of quality; it's almost a status symbol to have gen-uine dovetailed drawers, but they are more expensive, and I think they are a bit overrated. Dovetails look good and they do make an excellent connection, but drawers joined by other methods can be equally strong and functional.

Decisions, decisions—what kind of drawer should you use? I recommend solid wood or plywood; from there you're on your own. If you don't make the drawers yourself, compare the prices and construction methods of several door suppliers (many advertise in woodworking magazines).

CCF Industries (see Resources on pp. 157-159) makes drawers out of ½-in.-thick nine-ply Baltic birch ply-wood with ¼-in. plywood bottoms— and they're dovetailed. I've bought CCF drawers in unfinished knock-down form. They are reasonably priced, and they go together easily. The only drawback to the drawers is aesthetic: Those nine plies show on the top edges and dovetail ends (see the bottom drawer in the photo above).

New drawers (these are all from reface suppliers) are made of various materials joined in various ways. Shown here (from bottom to top) are a Baltic birch ply-wood drawer with ½-in. sides and dovetails, a soft maple drawer with ⅝-in. sides and dovetails, and a solid oak drawer with ½-in. sides and a locking dado joint.

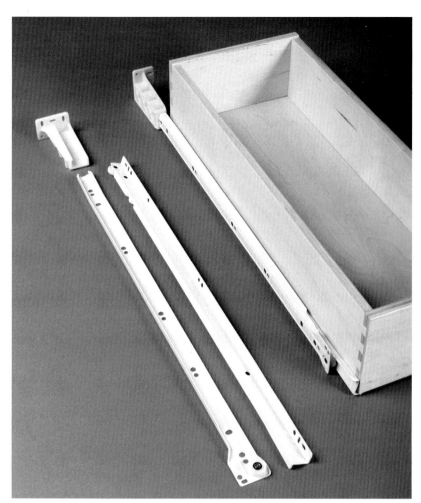

These Euro-style side-mount drawer slides are made of epoxy-coated steel with a plastic roller bearing. They can be installed in the course of a reface job, even on existing drawers.

Drawer slides

Even if you plan to retain the existing drawers in your kitchen, you should seriously consider upgrading the old hardware. Several manufacturers, including Amerock and Blum, make very similar versions of a side-mount slide with epoxy-coated (almond or white colored) steel runners and quiet-operating plastic roller wheels. These slides (see the photo at left) are inexpensive and durable. They have become the industry standard because they hold the drawer firmly in place and work reliably and smoothly on cargo loads up to 75 lb.

Side-mount slides are available in self-closing or non-self-closing types. Self-closing slides are more common. A ramped design in the back of the hardware pulls the drawer snugly shut when it's slid to within about 1 in. of the face of the cabinet.

Most slides are available in either three-quarter-extension or full-extension types. Full-extension slides are much less common because they are four to five times more expensive. They are also a bit more complicated to install. To illustrate the difference between the two, a Blum 550mm (22-in.) slide in three-quarter extension will pull out 17¾ in., whereas a full-extension model will pull all the way out of the cabinet, leaving a ⅝-in. space between the back of the drawer and the face frame. Full-extension slides are nice, but for most drawers, a three-quarter-extension slide is just fine.

Drawer sizes are specified by length, width, and height. The sizes you need will depend on the depth of the cabinet, the width of the opening, and the type of drawer slide you plan to use. If you're replacing old drawers and reusing the same slides, you can probably just measure the old drawers to get the sizes you need. But if you upgrade your slides, you'll want to refer to the new slide directions for drawer-sizing information (more about this on pp. 142-143).

For sizing and installation information, you should consult the slide manufacturer's instructions, but most three-quarter-extension slides have virtually the same specifications. Slide lengths are commonly available in 2-in. increments from 12 in. to 24 in.; some companies also offer shorter and longer versions. With old drawers, size the slide length to match the drawer as closely as possible. On new drawers, get the longest slides that will comfortably fit in the cabinet depth; 22 in. is a good slide length for most 24-in. deep cabinets. Size the length of the drawer to match the specified length of the slide. Also, be sure to get plastic mounting brackets for each slide. They fit over the end of the slide and mount to the back of the cabinet. Mounting brackets (see the photo on the facing page) come in right and left models (one for each side) and are purchased separately from the slides.

Many older cabinets have existing slides and drawer lengths that are less than the cabinet depth is capable of accommodating. This is one way to cut costs when you make new cabinets, but it's also a waste of good storage space. If your cabinets will accommodate deeper drawers, you might as well use them.

Drawer widths will need to be 1 in. less than the finished opening because the Euro-style slides take up ½ in. on each side. Old drawers typically have to be disassembled and cut down to reduce their width when outfitted with newer slides (see p. 144). Drawer heights should be about ¾ in. less than the height of the finished opening. Any taller than that, and you might not have enough room to get the drawer on and off the slides. Old drawers may have to be ripped down a bit.

The Amerock 9890 kidney lazy Susan has independently rotating plastic shelves and a center-post support. (Photo courtesy Amerock.)

Lazy Susans

Lazy-Susan shelves for corner base cabinets are available in full-round, pie-cut, and kidney-shaped versions. If you read pp. 40-43, you know I advocate removing pie-cut lazy Susans and replacing them with kidney-shaped Susans and a bifold overlay door.

Kidney-shaped shelves come in 24-in., 28-in., and 32-in. diameters (measured at their widest point). Although the shelves and parts can sometimes be purchased individually, they are usually bought as a kit that includes two or three shelves (two is more popular), a center-post support, and any other hardware needed for installation. Center posts telescope to accommodate various cabinet heights, so they are easier to install than non-adjustable posts.

The designs of lazy-Susan pivot mechanisms vary. You should get a center-post pivot that utilizes some sort of ball or roller bearing instead of a friction pivot. For shelves, the Amerock #9890 series (see the photo above) has

Door bumpers

Thickness of one door and a bumper

Kidney-shaped lazy Susan

Piano hinge

Traditional hinge

Figure the width of the doors as follows:

Determine the width of each half from the inside corner, then subtract the thickness of one door and a bumper (typically 7/8 in.) from each of the measurements.

independently pivoting ball-bearing-supported kidney-shaped shelves and an easy-to-adjust shelf stop. The stop holds the shelves firmly so the front of the shelf (the inside curve of the kidney) faces the opening and doesn't get in the way when closing the doors. Rev-a-Shelf makes similar shelving.

I've always used molded plastic shelves (white or almond) and have found them sturdy enough, but epoxy-coated wire-basket-type shelves and enameled steel shelving are other options.

If your existing lazy Susan is a pie-cut style, it's likely that the shelves are comparatively small (18 in or 20 in. in diameter) and that the back of the cabinet consists of a thin sheet of composition board curved to fit close to the shelves. If that is the case, you probably won't find a kidney-shaped

shelf small enough to fit in that space. So the thing to do is to remove the back and retrofit the cabinet to handle much larger shelves. A 32-in.-dia. lazy Susan will typically fit in the opened up space, and making the change is easier than you might think (see pp. 96-97).

When you are replacing a pie-shaped lazy Susan with a kidney-shaped unit and an overlay door, you'll actually be using two separate doors that are hinged together in the center. There are several different kinds of center hinges, but I've always used a basic full-length piano hinge. A 1½-in. by 36-in. piano hinge (brass or chrome) will do the job.

To figure the width of two-part lazy Susan overlay doors, use your master drawing (see p. 65). Number each half as a separate door, and keep in mind that you'll need to subtract the thickness of a door and bumper pad from each corner (see the drawing at left). Be sure to make it clear to your supplier that the doors are for a lazy Susan, and that you don't want a molded edge on the side of each door where the center hinge will go.

Full-round lazy-Susan shelving units are available in 18-in., 20-in., 24-in., 28-in., and 32-in. diameters, and can be found in plastic, wire, or steel versions. When replacing full-round lazy-Susan shelving, measure your existing shelf diameter and order accordingly. If it appears that you have extra room in the cabinet and can upgrade to a larger unit, do it. One thing you should be aware of is that a 32-in. full-round lazy Susan shelf will not fit through a typical base-cabinet door opening. To install one you will need to remove the countertop.

Tilt-out trays

If you like the idea of having tilt-out trays in front of your sink, you have a choice of tray types (see the photo at right). In cross section, most tray types are about 2 in. deep by 3 in. high, but lengths vary. Premolded plastic trays of different lengths are available in white or almond colors. It's also possible to get a long length of plastic tray with separate end caps; you cut the tray to the desired length, then glue on the ends. Or you can get stainless-steel trays, which come in 10 different lengths, ranging from 10 in. to 31 in.

Tilt trays can be purchased with hinges included, or you can buy the tray and hinges separately. A scissors-type tilt-out hinge is the most common style that's included in tray kits, but I've found they don't mount as easily or work as dependably as the false-front hinge style made by Feeny and shown in the bottom photo at right.

MOLDINGS

If you're refacing with wood doors, most reface-door suppliers can also provide you with several prefinished molding styles, and some will custom-make moldings. My major concern with moldings is that their color and finish match the new doors, so I usually buy my moldings from my door and drawer-front supplier. However, I often end up making a few small molding strips for various places. I've found I can get a respectable match on small or inconspicuous moldings, but don't want to take a chance on the bigger, more visible pieces.

For my own kitchen, I made basic squared-off moldings on a table saw. If I had wanted elaborate moldings like a crown or even a cove, I would have bought them unfinished from my local

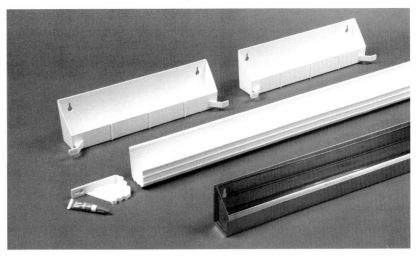

Sink-front tilt trays can be purchased as stainless-steel or plastic units of various sizes. There are also 36-in. tray extrusions, which can be cut and capped to form a tray of any desired length.

Hinges for tilt-trays come in two styles. The scissors hinge (two versions are shown at center and at right) is most common, but the Feeny brand (left) goes on more easily and works better.

lumberyard. Such moldings can typically be ordered in solid oak. Less expensive oak moldings are also available in several veneered varieties; they have a finger-jointed softwood base with an unfinished oak-veneer overlay and can pass for the real thing when installed. To purchase premade moldings in woods other than oak, you'll probably need to contact a custom millwork shop.

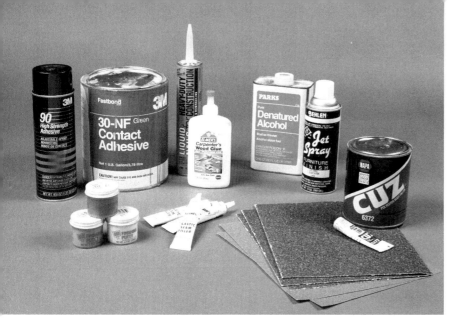

The adhesive you use will be determined by the type of veneer you decide to apply. A refacing job will also call for various solvents, sandpaper, filler, touch-up materials, and finishes. Most are available at large home centers.

Moldings are sold by the linear foot. Refer to the dimensions on your master drawing (see p. 65) to calculate how much you need. Molding lengths up to 8 ft. can be shipped without any trouble. Since I pick up my orders from my reface supplier when they're ready, I often get longer moldings by doing so if I can avoid having to join pieces. I also make it a point to order a bit more material than I expect I'll need, to make up for waste or mistakes. Yes, even professional craftsmen make cutting mistakes.

VALANCES

When ordering valances, I like to get them about 1 in. longer than I expect I'll need; that gives me some leeway for cutting and fitting (see p. 152). I usually specify a valance height of 6 in. because I think it looks "right" and it works well to conceal any lighting behind it. If I want to make my own custom valance design (see the drawing on p. 30). I order an unfinished wood board, cut my design, and send it back to get finished with the doors.

ADHESIVES

Using the proper glues in the proper places with the proper materials is of paramount importance when refacing. Common carpenter's wood glue (in conjunction with nails or screws) should be used to apply any wood extension strips to the cabinet face frames. And construction adhesive in a caulk-gun cartridge should be used to glue down any ¼-in. plywood pieces to the sides or bottoms of cabinets.

Phenolic-backed wood veneers and plastic laminate require a contact adhesive. Any contact cement suited for working with plastic laminate will suffice, but many refacers like to use 3M's Spray 90, which comes in an aerosol can. Although the product is solvent based and flammable (adequate ventilation is a must in the work area), the aerosol is particularly convenient to use, dries quickly, and doesn't smell bad. Contact adhesive is also the glue to use when gluing 10- and 20-mil flexible veneers that do not have a preglued back. A brush-and-roller grade of contact adhesive (solvent or water based) can be substituted, but the aerosol product is easier to use and has a higher initial grip.

Peel-and-stick veneers will stick to wood all by itself, but the bond may or may not be permanent. I use a water-based contact adhesive as a bonding agent. The material is brushed on the cabinet face frames and allowed to dry. This little-known procedure ensures a tenacious veneer bond. Many refacers don't use a bonding agent because it's an extra step in the process, but I consider it an essential step. Only a water-based contact cement should be used to "prime" wood prior to veneering; solvent-based glue will react with the veneer adhesive and destroy the bond. I regularly use 3M Fastbond 30NF and Lokweld H$_2$0 contact cement and have been pleased with both. One quart is usually plenty for a kitchen.

A water-based contact adhesive is also recommended for applying rigid-thermal-foil plastics because solvent-based adhesive can eat into the plastic.

MATERIALS FOR TOUCH-UP AND FINISHING

There are several other materials you'll need for cabinet refacing. I'll discuss many of them here and mention a few others later, when the need arises. Most of them are sold at hardware stores, building-supply stores, home centers, and through mail order.

Sandpaper of various grades is a necessity. Aluminum oxide 36-grit paper does an awesome job of sanding away excess body filler—and anything else that gets in its way. Grits of 80, 100, and 120 will also be needed.

Automotive body filler, available from auto-supply stores, is the product to use for filling holes, gaps, and cracks in the face frames prior to veneering. The filler comes with a small tube of hardener, and when the two are mixed together, the material sets up fast and hard.

If you're refacing with stained wood, you will want some matching stain to touch up prefinished veneer edges that have been sanded. It is best to use the same stain that was originally applied. Door makers can supply you with the proper concoction.

You'll need a clear spray finish to recoat any sanded spots. For this, most refacers use clear lacquer in an aerosol can. It's convenient, goes on nicely, dries almost instantly, and seems to adhere very well to any other finish. Clear spray finish is available in a gloss or satin sheen, and I recommend you get satin. If that ends up looking too dull for you, get the gloss and respray. I keep a can of each on hand at all times.

Some spray nozzles apply a better finish than others; I find the ones that deliver a fan spray pattern vastly superior. Some cans tout the fan-spray feature, while others, like the Behlen Jet Spray shown in the photo on the facing page, don't, but they still have it. The fumes from aerosol lacquers can be exceptionally noxious. It's a prudent safety measure to use a charcoal filter respirator when spraying any lacquer. Read the cans for all warnings, as well as directions.

To fill countersunk brad heads and any spaces between pieces of veneer that don't fit together perfectly (it happens) I use a color putty that is available at most home centers. The product is essentially white glazing putty with a color mixed in. If necessary (and it often is necessary), different colors can be mixed to get just the right shade for the job.

If you're working with plastic laminate, you'll want to have some laminate seam filler on hand. SeamFil, the product I use (see Resources on pp. 155-157), is a colored filler made specifically for filling joints between places of laminate. SeamFil is usually available from laminate suppliers and can be purchased in tubes to match any color or patterns of laminate.

5

PREPARING FOR REFACING

When you have all the materials on hand for your new kitchen, you are ready to roll up your sleeves and get to work. The first order of business is to prepare the work area, and that means emptying out the cabinets. Although you could leave everything in the cabinets and still do the refacing, it would be a bother because you would need to remove various items as you worked, and the cabinet contents would be guaranteed to end up covered with dust or touch-up spray finish. I always tell my customers that everything should be out of the cabinets, off the countertops, and preferably out of the immediate area before work begins.

If a new kitchen floor is part of the kitchen remodeling, I advise having it put in after the refacing is done. Then you don't have to worry much about heavy traffic or damage that could result from dropping tools and glue. If a new floor won't be going in (or if one has already been installed), take measures to protect it. First, lay down clean drop cloths, and over those place heavy cardboard pieces (salvaged boxes) or sheets of 1/8-in. Masonite,

and tape all the seams with duct tape. This work surface can be swept and vacuumed, and it can stay in place until the job is completed.

If new countertops are part of the job, I usually put them on after refacing (or, at least, after refacing the upper cabinets) and use the old counters as if they were a workbench. Otherwise, I place cardboard over the old counters and treat them as if they were brand new.

Dust is a major problem in any remodeling project, and while a reface job won't be as dusty as a complete kitchen tearout, it still generates some mess. To contain dust in the kitchen, hang drop cloths over any doorways into the room. A few staple-gun staples fired through the drop cloth and down into the top of the door casing will hold the cloth securely and not do any damage to the face of the molding.

When a kitchen is open to the rest of the house, there are no convenient doorways to seal off, but the dust can be contained if you frame up a simple and inexpensive friction-fit dust wall. Building a wall may sound like a lot of work, but it isn't; it usually takes less than 10 minutes to do. To make a dust wall you will need a few pieces of wood strapping (also known as furring strips) and plastic sheeting or drop cloths. Cut two lengths of strapping to span the distance you want to block off; those are the top and bottom plates. Then measure the height of the ceiling, subtract the thickness of the just-cut plates, add a little extra to the measurement (about ½ in.), and cut some strapping "studs" to that length. Cut one stud for each end of the wall, one to support any joints in the top plate (avoid joints there if possible), and one for every 4 ft. or so of wall span.

Now stretch out your plastic sheet or drop cloths and wrap them around the top plate a couple of times. If necessary, you can hold the material in place with a few staples into one side of the plate. Then lift the plate up to the ceiling where you want it to be (staple side down), and wedge the studs between the top and bottom plates. The frame will hold itself in place; there's no need for screws or nails. If the frame is a bit loose somewhere, you can tighten the fit by sliding a shim between the end of a stud and one of the plates. Let the sheeting hang down and, if needed, staple it to the framework. When the reface job is all done, the wall comes apart in a flash, no damage has been done, and you can reuse the strapping.

PREPARING THE CABINETS

Remove all the doors and drawers, latches, obsolete accessories, moldings, and valances. Strip everything that will be in the way right out of there all at once. Burn your bridges—there's no turning back. A screwdriver tip in a drill makes short work of this stage of the job (see the photo above right).

Begin by removing the old doors, moldings, drawers, and anything else that will be in the way of refacing.

If you are planning to reuse your old drawers, it's a good idea to label where they all went using the same numbers as on the master drawing (see p. 65), unless it's obvious. If you intend to reuse the existing drawer slides, you can leave them in place for now. Although they'll have to be removed when veneering the face frame, it's usually best to remove them as needed. That way, you won't

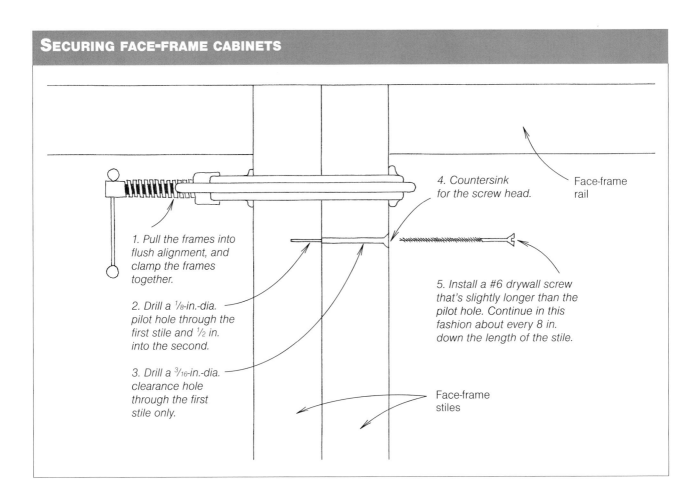

1. Pull the frames into flush alignment, and clamp the frames together.

2. Drill a ⅛-in.-dia. pilot hole through the first stile and ½ in. into the second.

3. Drill a ³⁄₁₆-in.-dia. clearance hole through the first stile only.

4. Countersink for the screw head.

Face-frame rail

5. Install a #6 drywall screw that's slightly longer than the pilot hole. Continue in this fashion about every 8 in. down the length of the stile.

Face-frame stiles

misplace the pieces, and it will be easy to remember exactly how they were installed.

Next, screw adjoining cabinet face frames to each other. If they are already well secured, leave them as they are. But I've found that most cabinets need at least a few screws to tighten up any looseness and close up small gaps between stiles. Sometimes you'll find that, although the frames are fastened together, the original installer didn't do a good job. The screws may be few and far between, or short and not gripping, or the face of the frames may not meet up flush to each other. Do what you can to make everything solid and flush along the front.

Securing cabinet face frames together is important, so I'm going to explain the process in detail. Before putting a screw in, push or pull as needed to align the front faces at the point where the screw will go, and clamp the stiles to hold them securely in position. If you find that it's extremely difficult (or impossible) to manhandle and screw face frames into flush alignment, then just do the best you can. Imperfect areas can be planed or sanded down later, or filled with auto-body filler; see pp. 99-101 for details. Use #6 drywall screws with a Phillips-head or square-drive head, and size them to go through one stile and about 1 in. into the other.

For each screw, make a pilot hole, a clearance hole, and a countersink before you drive it in (see the drawing on the facing page). Otherwise you'll split the wood or snap the screw. A keyless chuck in a drill makes bit changes easy and fast. Use a ⅛-in. drill bit to make the pilot hole, drilling through the first stile and about ½ in. into the second stile. Follow up with a ³⁄₁₆-in.-dia. clearance hole, which goes through the first stile only. If you hold a finger over the joint, you can feel the vibration of the bit as it exits the first stile and starts to cut into the second, and that's your cue to stop drilling (see the photo at right). Then make the countersink. Sometimes a countersink isn't required because the wood will be soft enough to allow screws to countersink themselves, but don't skip the drilling steps. If the screws seem to go in hard, rub some bar soap on the threads, or drive the pilot hole a little deeper, or both. If a screw doesn't grab, try a longer one. Work your way on down the length of the face frame, adjusting flushness as you go. I join standard wall or base cabinets with at least four screws. I want the cabinets solid as a rock when I'm done.

If more screws are needed at cabinet hanging rails or elsewhere to hold the cabinets more securely to the wall, this is the time to put them in. This is also the time to add new cabinets into the layout and to make any cabinet repairs, such as replacing a rotted sink base, or design modifications, such as adding a drawer (see the photo at right) or updating a lazy-Susan cabinet. These preliminary cabinet modifications can usually be done with a jigsaw, an electric drill, and basic hand tools.

Cabinets should be screwed (or rescrewed) together to make a solid foundation for veneering over. Drill a pilot hole and a clearance hole for screws. When you drill the clearance hole, your thumb can feel the vibration of the drill bit when it exits the first stile and starts to go into the second stile—that's when to stop drilling.

This rail is being added to a lazy-Susan cabinet to support a new drawer. It is fastened in with pocket holes on the back and stiffened with a backup block. Screws through the face frame are not a problem because they will be filled and veneered over.

Fixing a rotted sink base

One cabinet area that may need rebuilding is the sink base. It's not unusual for undetected plumbing leaks over the years to wreak havoc with the cabinet bottom. More than once I've had customers tell me they felt they should get new cabinetry instead of refacing because the floor of the sink base was rotted and disgusting. But I haven't yet encountered a cabinet that I couldn't rescue by cutting out the bottom, fastening cleats around the bottom edges, and fitting in a new 3/4-in. plywood floor. Another approach, if the existing floor is still substantially solid, is to layer a new floor of 1/4-in. plywood over the old. Plumbing pipes that go through the floor are an obstacle, but they can be dealt with. You can remove them temporarily (you might want to replace old parts anyway if a new sink is part of the remodeling), or you can work around them.

Converting to a kidney-shaped lazy Susan

If you will be converting a small and inefficient pie-cut lazy Susan to a bigger and more useful kidney-shaped lazy Susan (see the drawing on the facing page), do it before refacing. With the old pie-cut shelf unit and doors removed, you will typically be faced with a cylindrical cabinet back made of thin Masonite. The top and bottom of the cylinder are probably 3/4-in. particleboard. Take a hammer and, from inside the cabinet, knock the back loose from the top and bottom. It should come off easily and fall back into the dead space (which you're going to make better use of) behind the back of the cabinet. Pull the back out through the door opening and get rid of it. The bottom and top should remain securely in place.

Now measure and mark a line around the space, level with the top of the particleboard base piece, and fasten in cleats to the underside of the line. Next, measure and fit in a floor of 1/4-in. lauan plywood. The new floor will cover the old cabinet base and rest on the cleats. To get the new bottom in through the cabinet opening it may be necessary to slice it down the middle, and this can be done by scoring it several times along a straightedge with a utility knife. The 1/4-in. plywood is thin enough to work with easily, yet sufficient for the bottom because in this cabinet the bottom is mostly a filler and rodent barrier. The lazy-Susan pivot typically falls within the outline of the old bottom, so there will be plenty of support and material under the lauan for fastening into.

To install the new lazy-Susan shelves, set one shelf on the new floor and position it in the opening where you want it to be. I generally place it so the shelf front edges will be 1/2 in. to 3/4 in. away from the back of the door when it's closed. When it's in place, take a pencil and trace around the inside of the hole in the center of the lazy Susan where the support post will go. Now remove the shelf, eye up the center of the penciled circle, and make a mark. This will be the center of the bottom pivot. To find the top mark, hang a plumb bob inside the cabinet and jockey it around until the point zeroes in on the bottom pivot point, then mark the position of the top of the string. Attach the top and bottom pivot plates with screws. It's a bit of a trick getting the shelves and center post through the cabinet front and into place, but it can be done (you assemble the parts inside the cabinet).

Wall

Dead space

Cylindrical back of cabinet

Revolving shelves

Shelf pivot

Sides of adjoining cabinet

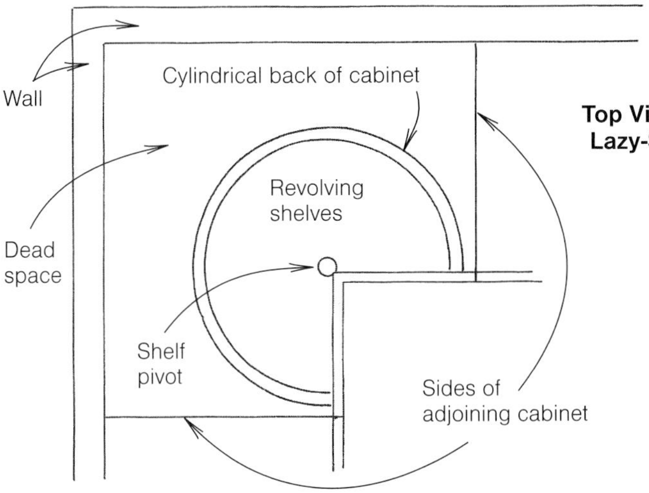

Top View of a Pie-Cut Lazy-Susan Cabinet

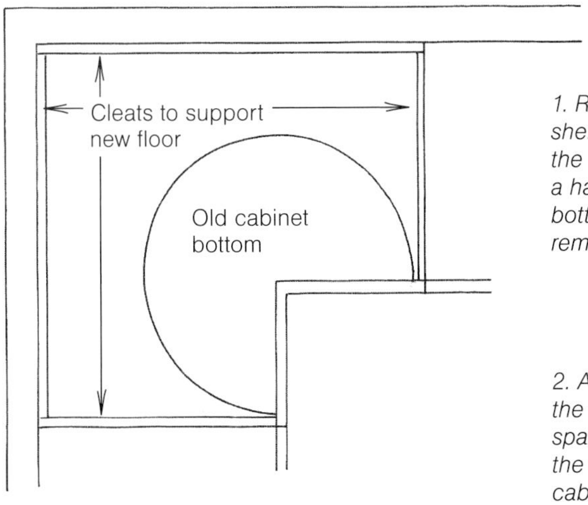

Cleats to support new floor

Old cabinet bottom

1. Remove the revolving shelves and knock off the cylindrical back with a hammer. The cabinet bottom and top should remain firmly in place.

2. Attach cleats around the perimeter of the space with the top of the boards level to the cabinet bottom.

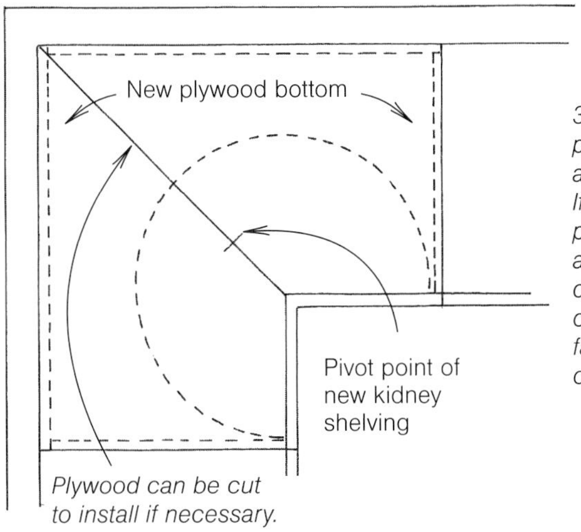

New plywood bottom

Pivot point of new kidney shelving

Plywood can be cut to install if necessary.

3. Cut a new $1/4$-in. plywood bottom to fit and fasten in place. If necessary, slice the piece down the center and rejoin inside the cabinet. The pivot point of the new shelving will fall over the solid wood of the old bottom.

Dealing with face-frame side overhangs

If your kitchen has face frames that overhang the sides of the cabinets (not all do), the frames will have to be trimmed flush with the sides of the cabinets before refacing can proceed. The overhangs can be removed with a hand plane, jigsaw, chisel, or router. A router equipped with a flush-trimming bit does the fastest and smoothest job, though it's also the loudest and messiest approach (see the photo at left). A ½-in. shank flush-trimming bit in a heavy-duty plunge router will do the best job.

Alternatively, if the side overhangs project ¼ in. or more (which they usually do), you can build the cabinet sides out with a piece of ¼-in. plywood (see the photo below left). Use construction adhesive and brads to fasten the sheet on, and then plane down any overhanging face-frame wood that extends past the plywood. The joint will soon be filled with body filler.

Before refacing, face-frame overhangs must be made flush with the sides. They can be trimmed with a router equipped with a ½-in.-shank flush-trimming bit (above). Alternatively, a piece of ¼-in. plywood can be butted up to the overhang (right).

Adding face-frame extension strips

Back in Chapter 3, I mentioned the need for face-frame extension strips, and now is the time to put them on. The strips are affixed to the inside edges of rails and stiles to ensure that doors and drawer fronts overlap the openings sufficiently (at least ¼ in.— ⅜ in. is even better). To figure out where the strips are required, use your master drawing and measurement calculation sheet (see pp. 64-69) to plot the layout of all doors and drawer fronts and the calculated reveals. Map out the dimensions right on the cabinet frames with a pencil. Then you can easily see where extension strips will be needed.

I use ¾-in. pine for extension strips. A pneumatic finish nailer speeds the work (see the photo at right). A little wood glue and some brads work well to fasten small strips, but screws work best on wider strips. In any event, use glue, and fasten the strips on flush with the front of the face frames.

FILLING AND SANDING THE FACE FRAMES

With all the repairs made and extension strips installed, holes and gaps need to be filled, and the surfaces will then have to be leveled and sanded smooth. Start by checking for areas where rails and stiles don't meet up flush to each other, and then make them flush. You can use a sharp block plane to get rid of any unevenness (see the photo below right). For minor irregularities, a sanding block outfitted with 36-grit or 50-grit sandpaper does a good job. There are times when it's impractical or too difficult to flush up adjoining pieces, and in those instances, just do the best you can. Auto-body filler can be used to finish up the leveling process.

Two-part auto-body filler (Bondo is one common brand name) is ideal for filling old screw holes, countersunk screw heads, gaps between face-frame pieces, and just about anything else. It is also the right stuff to feather out over slightly uneven face-frame pieces. The reason it's ideal is that it sets hard and fast. You can get body filler in any auto-supply store. One quart (the smallest container) is usually plenty for an average kitchen reface.

Extension strips are added to the face frames where needed. A pneumatic finish nailer is convenient for this task, but not necessary.

Any unevenness in the face frames can be leveled with a block plane.

Two-part auto-body filler is perfect for filling screw holes and other face-frame imperfections. Before use, you mix putty from the can with a hardener, which always comes in a tube.

Since auto-body filler cures quickly, you'll want to mix small quantities at a time. Follow the mixing directions on the can. The proportion of hardener to filler is not critical; less hardener results in a slower hardening time. I tend to use a bit more hardener than the directions call for, which, I understand, is also what happens in most auto-body repair shops. Mix the putty and hardener together on a clean, flat scrap of plywood, cardboard, or plastic laminate using a putty knife (see the photo above), and mix them thoroughly. Since the putty is usually gray and the hardener red, it's easy to tell when you've mixed them completely.

Before applying any filler, wipe the entire surface with a tack cloth or a rag dampened with denatured ethyl alcohol to remove any dust that would hinder the auto-body filler from sticking. Denatured alcohol should also be used to remove grease, which is commonly found near the stove. Grease will also prevent auto-body filler and veneer from sticking.

Dab the filler on and wipe it off; the process is similar to spackling drywall. You can use a wide taping knife to apply the filler if it's necessary (see the top photo on the facing page). Just remember that your objective is to fill and level imperfections, Although you want to overfill slightly, excess filler will need to be sanded off, and it doesn't sand as easily as drywall joint compound.

Auto-body filler cures to a rubbery stage and then gets hard. Sand off the excess after it hardens (in about five minutes). When I want to make quick work of removing excess filler I use 36-grit sandpaper (see the bottom photo on the facing page), but I always finish-sand with 100 grit. To maintain flatness, you'll need to use a sanding block, and be prepared to change paper often because the filler will clog the sheet quickly. Reputty any spots that don't get filled completely—there are usually a few.

While you're sanding the puttied spots, go ahead and give all the faces a once-over with 100-grit paper. Do this to give the surface a little tooth and level off any minor sanding imperfections. It is not necessary to sand to bare wood. Make a couple of sanding passes on the inside of the face frames, too. When all the sanding is done, clean off the dust with an alcohol-dampened tack cloth.

When the adjoining faces of stile pieces (or a stile and a filler strip, as shown here) are not perfectly flush, a layer of auto-body filler can be skimmed over the joint with a putty knife to level it all out (above). After it dries, any excess can be sanded smooth with 36-grit sandpaper (below).

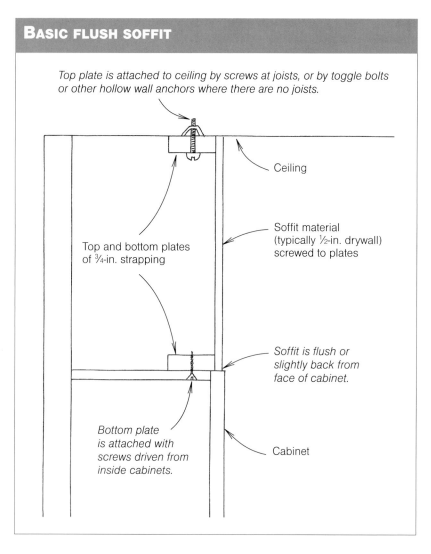

Top plate is attached to ceiling by screws at joists, or by toggle bolts or other hollow wall anchors where there are no joists.

Ceiling

Soffit material (typically ½-in. drywall) screwed to plates

Top and bottom plates of ¾-in. strapping

Soffit is flush or slightly back from face of cabinet.

Bottom plate is attached with screws driven from inside cabinets.

Cabinet

BUILDING A FLUSH SOFFIT

If your remodeling plans call for opening a closed soffit or closing an open soffit, the best time to get it done is before you start adding side panels and veneering face frames. If you're closing in a soffit, the simplest approach is to make it flush style (see pp. 30-31).

Begin by establishing the location of the top plate. Use a level to plumb up from the cabinet sides and fronts and all inside and outside corner points of the cabinet layout, and transfer the layout to the ceiling. If you'll be sheathing the side of cabinets with ¼-in. plywood, take that into account when making the marks.

From the established points, measure back the thickness of the drywall (or whatever material you intend to build the soffit out of) plus ⅛ in. for the backset, as discussed below. Then use a chalkbox to snap lines between all the marks. These lines are the layout lines for the top plate. A 2x4 will work for the plate, but ¾-in.-thick pine strapping is cheaper and is easier to work with.

Attach the strapping to the ceiling with drywall screws where there are ceiling joists to find purchase (see the drawing at left). When there is no solid wood, you can use some sort of hollow wall anchor. Put in enough fasteners to make the plate toe the line. On those pieces that aren't screwed directly into solid wood, I use some construction adhesive for extra hold.

Next, turn your attention to the bottom plate that will sit on the top front edge of the wall cabinets. Instead of snapping a layout line here, I just measure the backset of the plate with a tape or a gauge block as I go. When I do this, I make sure the soffit sheathing will end up back from the face of the cabinets about ⅛ in. I want extra backset because I always trim off this kind of soffit-to-cabinet joint with a molding, and if the soffit overhangs the front of the cabinets at any point, the molding won't fit flat (see the drawing on the facing page). The gap ensures that the molding will fit tight to the cabinets if it is fastened only into the front of the cabinets. A small gap at the top of the molding is rarely a concern because it can't be seen.

MOLDING AT CABINET/SOFFIT JUNCTURE

Molding

Soffit

⅛-in. backset

Set the soffit back slightly from the face of the cabinets. When nailed into the cabinets, the molding will fit nicely, and the gap at the top won't be visible.

Molding

Soffit

Cabinet

Problem
The "flush" soffit overhangs the cabinets, and the molding looks bad because it doesn't lie flat.

Molding

Soffit

Cabinet

Solution
You can circumvent the problem of an overhanging flush soffit by rabbeting the back of the molding.

Fasten the bottom plate with drywall screws driven down into the cabinet, or with screws driven up from inside the cabinet into the bottom of the plate. If you sheathe the soffit with ½-in. drywall, the top and bottom plates alone usually make a sufficient framework. Upright framing members (comparable to studs in a wall) are not necessary, except where sheets join and at corners. In these instances, strapping or 2x4 blocks can be installed as back-up cleats on the drywall; they need not be fastened directly to the framing.

Use drywall screws to fasten the drywall to the soffit frame. For outside corners, I don't use metal corner bead, which has to be nailed on. Instead, I use paper corner tape. Such a corner won't be as durable as one with a metal corner bead, but soffit corners don't need much protection. Spackle any drywall joints as needed. Wait until the cabinets are refaced before installing the soffit-to-cabinet molding strip.

Soffits built the way I've just described will not only go together quickly, but they'll also look great. This approach might seem lightweight compared to making a solid 2x4 or 2x2 framework, and it is. But in my experience, there are times when you need to build a good solid framework (for example, if you're going to hang peninsula wall cabinets from the frame), and there are times when it's okay to just throw up a couple of strips of wood, fasten some drywall on and be done with it.

Cabinet undersides don't
need to be covered, but if you
decide to cover them, use
¼-in. plywood (above). Cut
the new bottoms to fit, and
attach them to the bottom
frame of the cabinets with
glue and brads (right).

INSTALLING BOTTOM AND SIDE PIECES

If you've decided to cover the bottoms and sides of wall cabinets with ¼-in. plywood, you need to do it before you veneer the face frames. And if you intend to install ceramic tile on the wall underneath the cabinets, it's also a very good idea to put the bottoms on before the tile. Most cabinet bottoms are recessed, but they have a perimeter framework that hangs down, and that is usually sufficient material to fasten plywood into.

To install a bottom, hold the slightly oversized plywood piece in place (see pp. 76-77) and check its fit against the back wall. If necessary, cope the edge of the sheet for a better fit. Then trace the outline of the cabinet on the top (which is the back side) of the sheet. Cut along the line with a jigsaw, but leave the line and a little extra showing. Apply a bead of construction adhesive (see the top photo on the facing page), place the sheet into position, and nail it on using ¾-in. brads. A pneumatic brad nailer will make the job go much easier (see the bottom photo on the facing page).

After a sheet is glued and nailed in place, scrape away any adhesive squeeze-out and use a block plane to shave the excess plywood almost flush to the face frame. Then finish the job with 100-grit sandpaper in a sanding block. Another way to trim the edges is with a flush-trimming bit in a router (see the top photo at right), followed by sanding. When sanding, hold the block flat against the face frame; don't round over the the edge of the plywood. A sharp chisel and a steady hand will remove sections of plywood that the router or plane can't get to (see the bottom photo at right).

Excess plywood must be trimmed off, so the new bottom will be flush with the face frame. A flush-trimming bit in a router works beautifully for this job (above). In places where the router won't reach, you can use a utility knife or a sharp chisel (below).

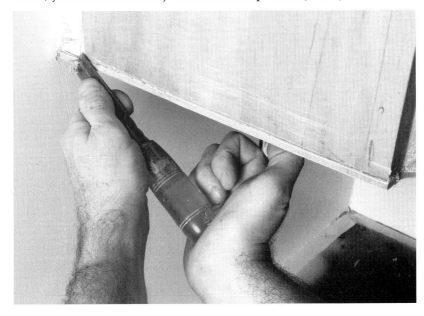

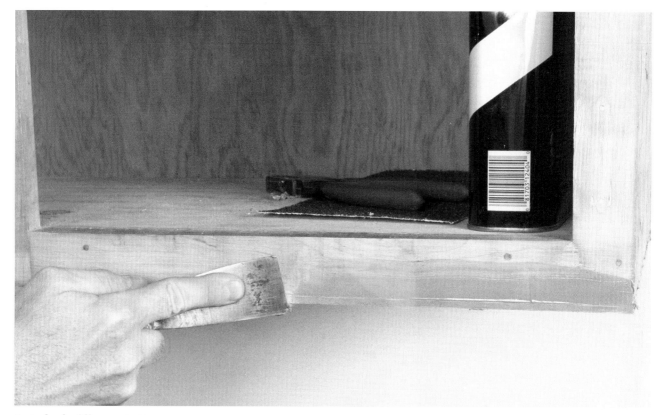

Auto-body filler seals the porous edge grain of plywood panels.

Side panels go on just like plywood bottoms: fit, fasten on oversize using construction adhesive and brads, and flush-trim the overhang. With plywood side panels I've found it's usually easier to mark and cut the bottoms to exact finished size instead of slightly over-size, and to get the best cut, I slice through the good face of the plywood with a sharp utility knife guided along a straightedge (a framing square).

After installing bottom and side ply-wood panels, I usually smear a layer of auto-body filler along the edge of the plywood where the veneer will go (see the photo above). This action seals the end grain, and, after sanding, makes for a smoother surface. When putting the auto-body filler down the edge, some of the filler will roll over on to the good face of the panel. When this happens, don't touch it—leave it there until it hardens. Then you can break it off without doing any harm.

If you use side panels of phenolic or three-ply veneer (see the photos on the facing page), they should be glued on with contact cement just like plastic laminate, and surface preparation is also the same (see Chapter 7). Phenolic veneer is cut and trimmed like plastic laminate, while three-ply veneer is cut with a utility knife.

Phenolic and three-ply veneers are glued to the cabinet sides with contact cement. Here, the surrounding areas are masked off to protect them from overspray.

Once in position, this slightly oversize sheet of three-ply veneer will be trimmed flush with the router.

6

VENEERING FACE FRAMES

There are three basic approaches that refacers take to veneering face frames (see the drawing on the facing page). The most commonly used method is to put the veneer only on the surface of the face frames; the inside edges do not get covered. This is, undoubtedly, faster and easier than other methods of veneering, and it looks just fine when the cabinet doors are closed. But when a door is opened, it is immediately evident that the cabinets have been refaced. Also, when only the surface is veneered, the inside edges of the veneer are more vulnerable to damage if banged into when items are taken out of the cabinet.

Another way to veneer face frames is to apply strips of veneer to the inside edges first, and then apply the face-frame pieces. With this method, the cabinets look just like new solid-wood face frames. You would have to be inside the cabinet, looking at the back side of the frame pieces, to realize that the cabinets had been refaced. But going to the trouble of gluing and trimming all those strips can be very time-consuming, and there is still a somewhat vulnerable edge seam where the two pieces meet.

The third veneer technique, and the one I'll focus on here, is to apply strips to the cabinet faces and wrap them around the frame so they cover the inside edges. My experience with 10-mil flexible veneers of oak, maple, and cherry is that they will all make the bend very well, and I suspect that other species of wood will perform similarly. I have always wrapped face frames when veneering because that's how I was taught to do it. It was only after a couple years of doing it this way that I realized wrapping the face frames is rare; some refacers I've talked to have never even heard of it. Others have heard of it but never tried it and have no interest in doing so because it strikes them as too much work. And some refacers offer veneer wrapping, but only as an upgrade option. It's too bad that wrapping the frames is not more common because, although it does take more time to do, it isn't difficult, and the result is a finished job that looks phenomenally better than other veneering methods. And a wrapped edge is much more resistant to wear and tear than an edge that ends right on the corner.

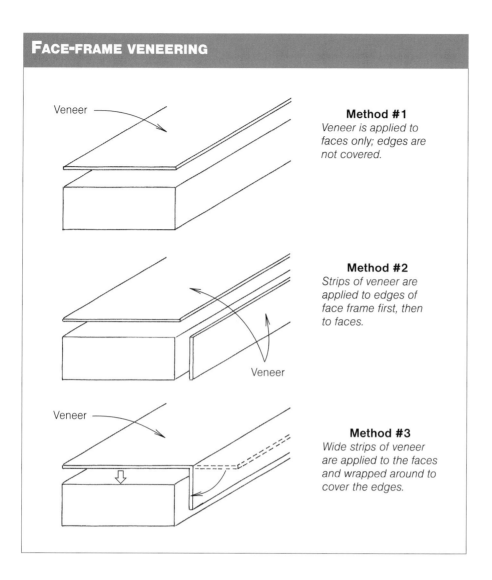

Veneer

Method #1
Veneer is applied to faces only; edges are not covered.

Method #2
Strips of veneer are applied to edges of face frame first, then to faces.

Veneer

Veneer

Method #3
Wide strips of veneer are applied to the faces and wrapped around to cover the edges.

Veneering is the part of refacing that many people find mysterious and intimidating. But like almost any other craft, once you see exactly how it's done, you'll realize that it's really not that difficult. This chapter will detail the steps I take for measuring, cutting, and applying veneer to cabinet face frames, and then I'll tell you how to put the finishing touches to it. In my work, I use pressure-sensitive (peel-and-stick) veneer, and that's what I'll be talking about in this chapter.

GETTING A GOOD BOND

Face frames must be prepared in order to get a good adhesive bond with the veneer. All refacers prepare the frames as described in Chapter 5, but some will do no more than that. Others take an additional step to ensure the best possible adhesive bond.

The worst way to apply veneer is to put it directly on unfinished wood or wood that has not had a bonding agent applied to it. Although the pressure-sensitive adhesive on the back of the veneer is quite tenacious, it works best on clean nonporous surfaces; glass, steel, and smooth plastic are ideal materials to bond veneer to. Wood that has been sanded and filled is not ideal. Veneer will stick to such surfaces reasonably well, but the bond is of dubious quality. Unfortunately, many reface jobs that have been done over raw wood have delaminated.

To reduce the risk of delamination, some refacers apply a coat of varnish or lacquer to seal the wood and provide a smoother, less porous bonding surface. Although I can't personally vouch for this method of face-frame preparation, I've talked to refacers who use it exclusively, and they report good results. But I think my way, which follows, is a lot easier.

I paint a bonding agent on the face frames prior to veneering. The bonding agent is nothing more than water-based contact cement applied with a brush. (Don't use a solvent-based adhesive; if you do, the bond will eventually fail.) Some refacers don't like to use a bonding agent because the stuff dries slowly (about 30 minutes). But the fact is that the bonding agent works excellently, and there's nothing difficult or particularly messy about using it, so I think that's reason enough to justify its application.

For the record, I have refaced more than 50 kitchens in the past five years, and out of those, I've had only two small spots of veneer come loose. Both failures were minor and on early projects, and the spots came loose shortly after I did the job; they can both be attributed to installer error (I was learning). In any event, I fixed them both

(I replaced one piece of veneer and used cyanoacrylate glue to stick down the other) and I haven't had any further problems.

MEASURING AND CUTTING VENEER

You can use various tools to cut flexible wood veneer, and I've tried most of them, but I always come back to a basic utility knife with a sharp blade. That's what I recommend you use too—at least while you are in the learning stage. In conjunction with the knife, I use a cutting board that I devised (see the sidebar on the facing page), a steel framing square, and a 4-ft. straightedge (my level).

Cut long lengths of veneer by marking the desired width on the sheet and cut it with a utility knife guided along a straightedge. If you're cutting an 8-ft. length of veneer, make as many marks as needed down the length of the sheet to index the straightedge guide. On dark-colored veneers, the marks will be easier to see if you make them on a piece of masking tape.

Do your cutting with the veneer face up. When cutting with the grain, the knife blade has a tendency to wander away from the straightedge if you don't pay close attention to what you are doing. Cross-grain cutting is more sure and easier to do. If your blade is sharp and you use firm pressure, you can make the cut in one pass, but sometimes you'll have to make a couple of cuts to get clear through the sheet. If the sheet of veneer has a blemish, such as a knot or a dark streak, don't use that part, or use it on a base cabinet, where it won't be obvious.

One of the first things I did after signing up my first kitchen refacing job was to make a veneer cutting board. This almost embarrassingly simple setup gives me a convenient surface to cut veneer on, and I'd be lost without it. You can make one in a few minutes, and I believe you'll be glad you did.

The board can be made of ¾-in. MDF, particleboard, or any other material with a homogenous composition—don't use plywood, which has a grain and can pull a knife blade off course. My board is 48 in. long and 26½ in. wide (see the drawing below), which is big enough to accommodate my framing square and a full-width sheet of veneer. Down the two long edges, I glued and nailed ¾-in. wide strips of ¼-in.-thick pine. These form raised edges that act as a fence to rest the veneer and my framing square against when making cuts.

I set the cutting board on sawhorses right in the kitchen where I'm working (see the photo below), and when I'm not using it to cut veneer, it doubles as a convenient workbench. That's about all there is to a cutting board. I told you it was simple.

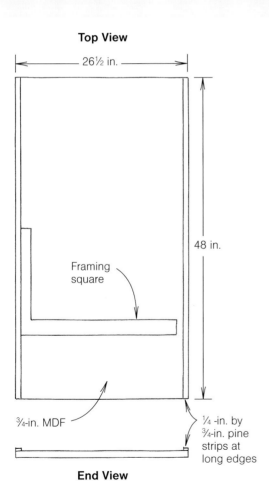

Top View

26½ in.

48 in.

Framing square

¾-in. MDF

¼-in. by ¾-in. pine strips at long edges

End View

With a cutting board set up in the work area, face-frame veneer pieces can be cut to the slightly oversize dimensions that will be needed. Here a sheet is being cut into thirds for ease in handling.

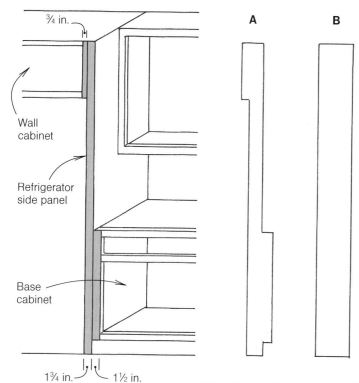

¾ in.

Wall cabinet

Refrigerator side panel

Base cabinet

1¾ in. — 1½ in.

A   B

This layout calls for a single piece of veneer to cover the stile of a wall cabinet, the stile of a base cabinet, and the full-length face of a refrigerator side panel.

Rather than cutting a complex shape (A in the drawing above), simply add the width of the three faces (4 in.) to the amount needed for wrapping the stiles (¾ in. on either side) plus ¼ in. extra on each side, and cut a single-width strip of veneer to that size (6 in.), as shown in B.

strip, just add ½ in. to the width of the face-frame front and any edges it will cover. For example, a 1¾-in.-wide stile on a cabinet with a ¾-in.-thick face frame would call for a veneer piece that is 3¾ in. The ½ in. gives you a margin for error in placing the strip. You can certainly add on more than ½ in. if you want, but don't go less until you're comfortable with the process. Be aware that along one length of most veneer sheets, there is no adhesive for about ¼ in., so you won't want to include that in your layout.

Single pieces of veneer should cover adjoining cabinet stiles. For example, if you have two cabinet stiles with a filler sandwiched between them, you don't cover each one with a separate strip of veneer; one piece takes care of all three. To my mind, one of the great things about refacing is getting rid of all those joints.

Wherever possible, simplify the shapes you'll be cutting. For example, where short cabinets meet longer cabinets, cut the full length of veneer to the widest width you'll need (see the drawing at left). This will result in some waste, but it gives more stiffness to the veneer and makes cutting and installation easier.

With the longest stile pieces cut to size, you'll find (in most instances) that all the remaining vertical strips are less than 32 in., which happens to be one-third of a 96-in.-long sheet. So to make the cutting easier, I usually cut the sheet into thirds. However, I only cut sections off as I need them. I do all sheet ripping and cutting to length on my cutting board set over sawhorses.

Start by measuring and cutting all the vertical pieces of veneer (for the cabinet stiles) that will be needed to do the job. If any especially long pieces are required, say, for on a tall oven or pantry cabinet, cut those out first.

Cut to width first and then to length. Strips should be cut about ½ in. wider and longer than they need to be. To determine the width of a given veneer

As you cut the vertical strips to size, set them in the cabinets near where they will go. To avoid confusion, you might want to note their location on the backs of the strips with a marker pen.

VENEERING THE STILES

When all the vertical strips are cut, turn your attention to putting them on (the horizontal pieces, for the rails, will be cut later). But before you can apply the veneer, you need to brush on the water-based contact-cement bonding agent and let it dry. I usually apply it before I cut the veneer pieces so it will be dry (or nearly dry) about the time the veneer pieces are ready to use. You may or may not want to be so efficient in your early learning stages.

The contact cement can be applied with an inexpensive disposable bristle or foam brush (see the photo above right). Put bonding agent only on the faces and edges of stiles that will be covered. Try not to slop adhesive onto the adjacent rails; a little bit of overlap is okay but not a lot.

Next, make a couple of veneer alignment marks at the top and bottom of the face frame. If you will be wrapping the veneer to cover the edge of a typical ¾-in.-thick face frame and you have figured ½ in. of extra width on the veneer, you are aiming for ¼-in. overage on each side. So you make the reference marks on the rail 1 in. from the edge of the stile (see the photo at right). It's only necessary to do this on one side.

Finally, after all the careful preparation, it's time to put on a piece of veneer. To do this, peel back about 1 in. of the protective paper backing at the top of

For a strong bond with the veneer, first apply water-based contact cement to the face frames, including the inside edges where the veneer will be wrapped.

On a ¾-in.-thick face frame, reference marks on the top and bottom rails 1 in. away from the stile will help in aligning the veneer piece.

To apply a length of veneer, peel back the protective paper about 1 in. and lightly stick the top on, making sure it's aligned with the reference mark (above). Then, while holding the bottom of the veneer against the bottom reference mark (right), slowly peel the paper backing down and out from under the veneer. Stop at intervals to pat the veneer into place.

the strip, hold it so that just a bit hangs over the top of the face frame (something like an overhanging soffit will require that you butt directly into it) and align one top edge with the top alignment mark on the rail (see the photo above left), then lightly stick the top down. Align the bottom edge of the veneer with the bottom mark, pat

the top firmly in place, and, while still holding the bottom in position, slowly peel the paper backing out from underneath the piece (see the photo above right). Stop at intervals to pat down the veneer as you go. This procedure works a whole lot better than peeling the whole piece of paper off the back and then trying to position the piece, which is what I did when I first started using veneer (and I screwed up more often than I care to recall). Long pieces are much easier to put on if you have a helper—one person holds one end in position while the other person holds the other end, and then one of them slowly peels off the paper backing and presses down the veneer. If you're working alone, you can usually hold an end in place with a spring clamp.

When the veneer is properly positioned, pressure should be applied over the entire surface with a wood or steel roller. Rubber laminate rollers are not recommended because they do not deliver the concentrated pressure of a harder material. An inexpensive wallpaper seam roller (made of wood) will do the job. Alternatively, you can apply pressure with a scrap of ¼-in. Masonite that has been belt-sanded to a blunt point. I use a smoothing tool I developed and dubbed a "Veneer Slick." It's nothing more than a block of wood that holds a ¼-in.-thick piece of UHMW (ultra-high molecular weight) plastic. The plastic is very hard, yet "slippery," and can be swiped over prefinished veneer without doing any damage. The Veneer Slick is more manageable than a roller and can smooth into corners, where a roller won't go. Most veneer manufacturers actually recommend a smoothing tool over a roller. You can make your own smoother, get them from some tool catalogs, or get the Veneer Slick from me (see Resources on pp. 155-157).

A smoother is pressed down and drawn slowly over the veneer. One solid swipe is usually enough to flatten

the veneer, squeeze away air pockets, and set the bond (see the photo above). If you are concerned about scratching the prefinished veneer surface with a scraper, do the smoothing over waste pieces of the veneer paper backing.

Veneer should be rolled with a hard-surface roller (not rubber) or pressed down with a smoothing blade. This Veneer Slick has a blade of "self-lubricating" plastic, and can be swiped over finished veneers without doing damage.

Stile pieces have to be sliced free at the rails (right). Do this with a utility knife. Once cut free, the veneer can be wrapped around the edge (below) and pressed down tightly.

With the veneer in place and firmly adhering to the face frames, it's time to wrap the edges. But before the material will wrap you'll need to slice it where it meets the top and bottom rails. This is best done with a utility knife. Hold the blade of the knife flat against the edge of the rail and slice up to the stile (see the photo above). Start with the point of the knife against the veneer and push it into the veneer, as if you are sawing with the blade, but cut only on the push stroke. When you make these cuts at the top and bottom rails, you end up with a flap that can be folded in. Wrap the flap tightly around the edge and smooth it (see the photo at left). Use the edge of your smoothing tool to push the veneer tight into the top and bottom corners. Don't worry if the veneer cracks a little as you wrap it. That's normal, and it's not a problem. We will tend to it after all the veneer is on.

After the veneer is wrapped, the veneer "ears" that overhang onto the rails must be removed. One way to do this is with a straightedge and a knife.

After the veneer is folded, two veneer "ears" are left on the top and bottom rails, and they must be removed. To do this, hold a straightedge against the edge of the just veneered stile so that it extends over the ear, and cut the veneer off by slicing it with a knife down along the edge (see the photo above). If you didn't overpaint the bonding agent too much, severed ears should lift right off. Any dry adhesive that remains under or near the cut should be rubbed off with your finger.

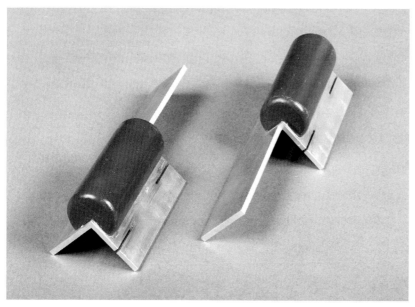

These multiple-use tools (MUTs) were devised by the author for removing veneer ears and doing other veneer refacing tasks.

A MUT in ear-removal mode. The tool is configured to key easily into position, and you slice along the long edge.

⌐ see note:

For years I removed ears by trimming along a straightedge, but after a while I developed another specialty tool, the refacer's MUT (multiple-use tool) shown in the photos at left, which serves as a guide for these amputations, as well as other veneer cuts that I'll discuss shortly. The tools are made from 1½-in. angle iron and a dowel; on the short side, the metal is notched on each end ¾ in. from the corner.

After veneering stiles on outside corners that have a side panel, you will need to trim off the veneer overhang using a utility knife. On my early attempts to remove this veneer overlap, I pared it down with the knife, but this is tedious, and it's also difficult to do because the blade often tracks off course in the irregular grain of the wood. The best way to make the cut is to score the paper back of the veneer (see the top photo on the facing page). Work carefully, and make sure the knife blade point is sharp. Hold it in the corner against the cabinet side, and score two or three times, then bend the veneer back and forth (gently at first) until it breaks free. The break should be fairly clean, but there will be some roughness. Don't worry about sanding it smooth until after all veneering is done.

If you can get to the back of excess veneer pieces that overhang at the top and bottom of the face frame, score their backs and break the pieces off (see the bottom photo on the facing page). If you can't get to the back side, lay a straightedge over the face as a guide to cut the veneer.

Veneer that hangs over the edge of a side panel is best removed by carefully scoring the back of the paper, then flexing the veneer to and fro until it breaks off.

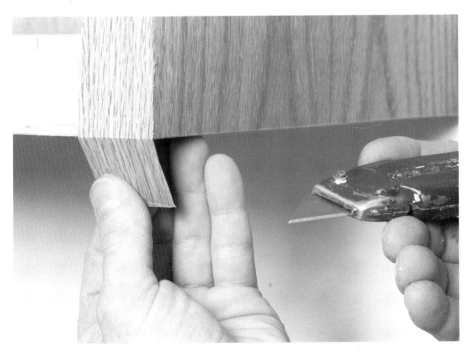

Excess veneer at the top or bottom of the face frame can be scored on the back side and flexed back and forth until it breaks.

It's not easy to trim excess veneer off flush with the back side of the face frames. A utility knife used with a MUT makes for a faster, more accurate job.

When applying veneer on stiles that meet at inside corners or up against walls, hold the strip in place where it will go before you remove the backing paper. That way you can check on how it will look and scribe it for a better fit if necessary.

Don't try to use one wide piece of veneer bent in the center to cover both cabinet stiles that meet at inside corners—it doesn't work out very well at all. A separate piece of veneer needs to be applied to each stile, one after the other (it doesn't matter which side goes on first). Inside corners, particularly 45° inside corners, are somewhat difficult to veneer. The thing to know here is that an imperfect matchup of the two veneer edges in the corner is usually the rule. With experience, your

ability to join veneer pieces in the corners will get better, but even the best refacers admit that some gap in the fit is often unavoidable. Any imperfections will be filled later with color putty (see pp. 128-129).

After wrapping veneer around the inside edges of the face frames, there should be some excess veneer that extends beyond the frame into the cabinet. If you can conveniently score the back side of this veneer with a knife and snap the excess off, do so. If not, you can slice off the extra material by cutting it from the face, but it's hard to make a good cut this way. Another option is to use the MUT, which has a slot in it that accepts the point of the utility knife and keeps the blade from wandering off course as you draw the two tools along (see the photo at left). Later, the back edges can be sanded.

VENEERING THE RAILS

Rail pieces are laid out and cut just like the stile pieces. You start with the longest pieces first, cut all the pieces that you'll be needing at the same time, and place them in the cabinets where they will go. Measure the rails (including the parts that will be wrapped) and cut the pieces ½ in. wider than needed. As for length, make them 1 in. or so longer than necessary. Each piece will be custom cut to exact size as it's installed.

Brush on the contact-cement bonding agent, being careful not to get it on the newly veneered stiles. But if a little bit does get on the veneer it's okay (providing it is prefinished) because it rubs off fairly easily after it's dried. (If the veneer isn't finished, the glue will still come off, but not without some effort.) Most cabinet bottom rails meet flush to the cabinet bottom, and when this is the case, I stick a length of ¾-in. masking tape down on the cabinet bottom at the back of the rail. The tape lets me paint the edge without worrying about over-runs into the cabinet (see the photo at right). I usually leave the tape in place until the rail has been veneered and trimmed.

When the contact cement has dried, you can start veneering the rails. Here the challenge is cutting the veneer pieces to precise length so they fit per-fectly. There are a couple of ways to do this. One is to cut the pieces to exact length before sticking them down. Using your cutting board and square (see the sidebar on p. 111), cut about ¼ in. off the end of the strip with a utility knife. Make sure the blade is sharp and make a clean slice (see the photo at right). Take this piece of veneer and hold it on the face frame, parallel with the rail, with the square-cut end seated in place against one side. At the other end, take the sharp knife and push down on the veneer precisely where it meets and overlaps the stile veneer (see the photo below right). This will make a tiny nick exactly where you want to cut the piece off. Now index the veneer back against the edge of the cutting board, hold the knife on the nick mark, slide the square up to the knife, and make a clean cut. Hold the veneer back in place on the rail and check the fit. It should be perfect.

Where bottom rails meet flush to cabinet bottoms, a length of mask-ing tape inside the cabinet keeps the bonding agent from slopping onto the cabinet bottoms.

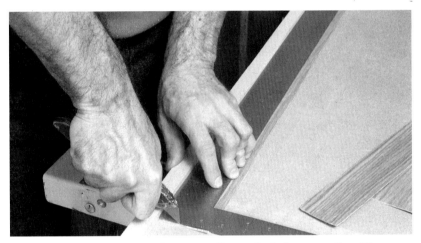

Rail pieces of veneer must be cut to fit precisely between the stiles. Start by square-cutting one end of the veneer with a framing square on the veneer table (above), then hold the piece on the rail with the square-cut end in position, and make a knife nick where the other end meets the stile (below). Take the piece back to the cutting board to make the final cut.

For rail pieces, reference marks must be made on masking tape, not on the stiles, which have already been veneered.

Before gluing the veneer in place, you need to make two reference marks about 1 in. away on the stile, just as was done when gluing veneer on the stiles. This time though, make your marks on small pieces of masking tape instead of directly on the veneer (see the photo above).

Apply the veneer piece just as you did on the stiles: Peel back about 1 in. of the paper backing, butt the piece up tightly to the stile, stick it down lightly, make sure it is in line with the reference marks on both ends, then slowly peel and stick. You'll find out just how precise your cut was when you get to the other end. If the veneer is a tad

too long, trim it in place; don't try to jam it in or pound it down. If it's a tad too short, you'll fix it later with color putty. If the fit is dead perfect and it's your first time fitting a rail piece, you can pat yourself on the back because it usually takes a few tries to get the hang of fitting tight rail pieces. That's why it's a good idea to put your first pieces of horizontal veneer on an inconspicuous base cabinet, not on wall cabinets at eye level.

Another way to fit rail veneer pieces is to square-cut one end and stick the veneer on, letting the other end overlap onto the stile. Then cut it to fit using the refacer's MUT. The

When one piece of veneer butts into another, as on rail pieces or this center stile, square-cut and butt one end and stick the piece on so it overhangs on the other end. Then cut it in place, using the MUT as a guide.

same technique would be used for center stiles (see the photo on the facing page).

You can wrap horizontal veneer without any additional work (since no ears remain), and then trim off any excess at the back. When wrapping veneer on bottom rails that meet flush to a cabinet bottom, you need to trim the excess away very neatly, because a bad cut will be clearly visible. However, since the rail is flush, there's no guide or reference for making a good cut. When this is the case, you can rig up a straightedge guide for the knife or simply use the knife-slot guides of the MUT (see the photos on p. 124).

see notes

(see the photos on p. 124)

WHAT IF YOU GOOF?

If you put a piece on crooked or too short, you have to take it off right away. Removing veneer while the glue bond is fresh is much easier than after the adhesive has had a chance to cure (ultimate adhesion strength is reached in approximately three days). Get the veneer off any way you can. Pull, pick, scrape and rub off every last vestige of the material and the adhesive under it. The veneer and paper back will often come off, leaving the adhesive for you to struggle with. A rag soaked in mineral spirits will help loosen the glue. I guarantee that if you end up having to remove one piece of veneer, you'll be very careful not to let it happen again. However, if you do make another mistake, don't feel bad, because everyone does sooner or later.

To get a neat cut on the inside of bottom rails, use a MUT (or a straightedge) to guide the knife blade.

note: simple cuts, but go slow on in increments.

Once the cut has been made, the excess veneer can be pulled up, and the masking tape comes along with it.

FINISHING TOUCHES

When all the veneer is on, the face frames will look pretty good. But they'll look a whole lot better after some sanding and touch-up work.

Sanding the edges

I use a full sheet of 100-grit sandpaper folded in quarters (no sanding block) to sand outside edges where a veneered front meets a side or bottom panel (see the photo at right). Sand very lightly at first into the edge and toward the wall behind. Sand only on the edge of the veneer, not on the cabinet side or veneer face. The objective is to remove excess material, and no more. If you use a light touch at first, you won't find this a difficult thing to do. As a final sanding, stroke down the edge a couple of times. The result should be a crisp, tight corner that is remarkably good looking (see the photo below right). A close inspection will reveal that the edge actually is rounded a bit, but it's only the thickness of the veneer that's rounded. For all practical purposes, the corner is square.

Another important area to sand is where the veneer wraps around the inside of the face frames. Hairline cracks invariably develop at this point, and some refacers leave them this way, particularly with close-grained woods like cherry and maple, which crack relatively little compared to oak. I think it's much better to smooth the edges. Using 100-grit or finer paper, sand the

Use 100-grit sandpaper and a light touch to smooth the rough-cut outside edges of the veneer.

After sanding, the outside edges should look crisp.

Sand wrapped edges only enough to smooth the bend, not so much that you sand through the veneer into the paper backing.

The rough-cut edges on the back side of the frame won't be seen, and some refacers don't sand them at all. If you wish to go the extra mile, a quick pass with an oscillating detail sander will smooth the wood.

veneer bends to smooth them (see the photo at left). Use a light touch, and sand only the outside of the curve. When that much is smooth to the fingertips, stop sanding. You will have sanded off the finish and stain color, but you won't have gone into the paper backing of the veneer. If you are leery about sanding corners, veneer some scrap blocks of wood and practice sanding on them. You will find it's easy to do a good job.

After sanding all the outside edges, you will be tempted to leave the rough-cut back edges of the face-frame veneer the way they are, and I wouldn't fault you for it; after all, they are inside the cabinet and out of sight. But if you want to do an exceptionally good job, sand the back edges, too. I use an oscillating detail sander with 50-grit or 80-grit paper for this (see the photo below left). Such a tool would be too aggressive and difficult to control on outside edges, but it makes short work of inside edges, where the main idea is to level and smooth the wood. Afterwards, I round the edge slightly with 100-grit paper, sanding by hand.

Touch-up staining

If the veneer was stained, now is the time to restain all the sanded edges. Mix the stain thoroughly and apply it with a cloth or foam brush. The stain will end up getting on the finished face frames as well as the bare wood, but don't let it dry there; wipe off the stained face frames with a soft cloth right after applying the stain. Make sure to wipe some stain over all rail-to-stile butt joints, too, as well as down inside-corner joints. Give the freshly stained edges a few minutes to dry before spraying on a clear top coat, as discussed on the facing page.

Removing stray contact cement

One more thing to get done before the top coat goes on is to remove any bits of contact cement that got on the veneer during the veneering. If you wiped stain on the frames, the solvent in that usually softens up the glue spots so they can be easily rubbed off when the frames are wiped down. Otherwise, use a rag dampened with mineral spirits to soften and remove any stray deposits of contact cement.

Spraying the edges

The freshly sanded edges need to be recoated with finish. I apply three or four light coats of aerosol spray— sometimes more, if I feel it's needed (see the photo at right). I hold the can about 5 in. away from the edge, and I make sure it's moving while spraying. So there is some order to my technique, I always try to spray all the stile edges first, then go back through and spray the rail edges. Lacquer, which is what I've always used, dries very quickly; usually, by the time I have sprayed all the stiles in a section of cabinetry, they've dried enough that I can go back to where I started and spray the rails. And I can continue to repeat this spray pattern until I have all the coats on that I want. Of course, when you do this spraying, you're effectively coating the entire face frame because of the wide spray pattern, but that's okay; it will work out just fine. You should wear an appropriate vapor respirator when spraying lacquer, or at least get some cross-ventilation in the room by opening some windows. When I'm done spraying, I take a break, go breathe some fresh air and let the lacquer dry for 10 or 15 minutes before the next stage—puttying the brad holes and the joints.

Spray freshly sanded edges with several light coats of aerosol lacquer.

REFACING WITH WASHED FINISHES

If you will be refacing with veneer that has a washed finish (see pp. 11-12), you can applying it just as you would any other veneer, except that you might not want to wrap the face frames. I've done only one washed-finish reface job, and I found that wrapping did not work well because I couldn't stain and finish the edges to my satisfaction (the stain flaked off in good-size pieces when the veneer was wrapped). So I veneered just the front of the frames, and painted the inside edges. It worked out fine. The finished kitchen looked beautiful—and it still does.

However, I have since learned that some white stains and finishes can be wrapped and finished off with success, so my one experience should not necessarily deter you from wrapping a washed veneer. Consult with your supplier or experiment by wrapping and finishing some sample blocks before you make a decision on which way to proceed. You might also consider using plastic laminate to finish face frames with washed doors. Though I've never seen this, I've heard it's done. Working with plastic laminate is discussed in Chapter 7.

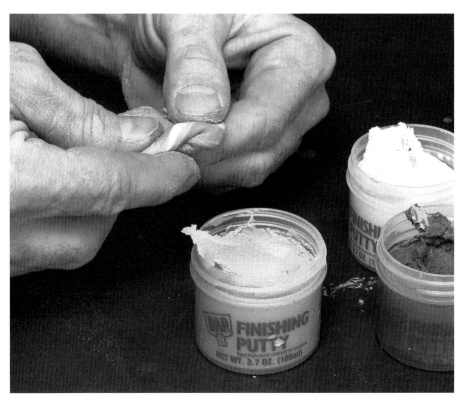

To get the best wood match with color putty, custom-mix small quantities with your fingers.

Puttying

Brad holes and all joints between joining pieces of veneer need to be puttied. I take puttying seriously. Many refacers find a color of putty that's "close enough" and use it, but a conscientious refacer will mix different colors together to get the best color match. Do this a bit at a time by kneading the two (or more) colors together with your fingers (see the photo above). You can gauge the quality of a color match by holding a blob of the stuff on your finger at arm's length against the veneer, closing one eye, and squinting with the other. (This method not only works, it looks very professional and will impress anyone who sees you do it.) I try to place brads in small knots or darker areas of the wood (if such areas are available) because it's easier to blend in a dark putty color than a light one.

On flat areas you can apply the putty with your fingers (see the top photo on the facing page). Even if joints are tight, smear some putty over them. For inside corners I've found I can apply a wonderful-looking small fillet of putty by smearing a line of the substance into the corner and then swiping down through it with the tip of a fine ($\frac{1}{32}$-in.) nail set (see the bottom photo on the facing page). Any residue that remains on the edge can be scraped off.

Smear the putty on every joint with your fingers (above). Even if the veneer pieces meet tight, the color putty will make the joint look better. On inside corners (below), form a fillet of putty, then use the edge of a nail set to scrape away excess putty.

Color putty leaves a cloudy film around where it has been applied, and this must be wiped off. Use a cloth lightly dampened with mineral spirits to wipe off the spots, and then follow up by hand-buffing the frames with a clean, dry cloth. Sometimes I go one step further and spray another thin coat of lacquer over the edges, and then again, sometimes I don't. Either way, at this point you're done with the refacing, and you're ready to put on the new doors.

7

REFACING WITH PLASTIC LAMINATE

If you have decided to cover your old cabinets with flexible wood veneer, you can skip this chapter and go straight to Chapter 8. But if you plan on using plastic laminate, this chapter will give you enough information to get you started. Readers who want to delve further into the subject may want to consult my book *Making Plastic-Laminate Countertops* (The Taunton Press) for a thorough description of the tools and techniques for working with plastic laminates.

The process of refacing with laminate is similar to refacing with wood veneer. You cover the bottoms and sides of the cabinets first, then the face frames. For the face frames, you have a choice of two methods: You can apply one large piece to a long run and then rout out the openings (sheet laminating), or you can apply individual pieces (strip laminating).

There is one very important laminate fabrication rule: The laminate must be stored in the area where it will be worked for at least 48 hours prior to using it. The time is needed to allow the material to acclimate to the temperature and humidity of the working environment. If you ignore this rule, you invite disaster. Laminate pieces

that appeared to be sticking well after you glued them on may suddenly come loose a few months (or sooner) down the road. And if the laminate will be glued to ¼-in. lauan plywood (more about this on p. 132), it's equally important that the plywood be given the same preconditioning.

TOOLS

Plastic laminate is a very different material than flexible wood veneer, and you need some special fabrication tools to cut, apply, and finish it. The ones I find most useful are shown in the top photo on the facing page.

An inexpensive carbide scoring tool can be used for rough-cutting sheets of laminate to size. The scoring tool consists of one pointed carbide tooth on the end of a handle. To use it, you lay a sheet of laminate on a clean surface with the good side up, then pull the tooth over the laminate, using a straightedge as a guide. The tooth scrapes a little furrow in the surface. After scoring two or three times, hold down on one side of the sheet and lift up on the other, and the sheet will break cleanly along the cut. (Don't bend the scored sheet down to make the snap because it will not break cleanly.)

Refacing with plastic laminate calls for some specialized tools. Shown here (clockwise from top right) are a laminate trimmer outfitted with a flush-trimming bit, a pair of laminate snips, a carbide scoring tool, a laminate roller, a laminate hand file, a Laminatrol cutting guide, and a hand slitter.

Laminate sheets can also be cut with laminate snips, which work something like metal shears. The snips are easier to use than the scoring tool, but they cost a bit more, too.

One quick way to cut many strips of laminate to precise size (as you would want to do when strip-laminating a face frame) is to use a table saw equipped with a fine-cutting carbide sawblade. If you go this route, I highly recommend that you get a Laminatrol cutting guide (see Resources on pp. 155-157). This inexpensive aluminum extrusion keeps the laminate from lifting up or sliding under the table saw's fence when you rip strips (see the photo at right).

A Laminatrol cutting guide fits under the fence of a table saw and allows for controlled cutting of strips.

Another strip-cutting tool is the laminate hand slitter, which has two steel wheels that slice the material as you push or pull the tool along a straight edge of laminate (see the photo at left). The tool is portable and doesn't make any noise or throw chips. Models vary in width of cut; mine adjusts to make cuts from ¼ in. to 3¼ in. The only real drawback to a hand slitter (besides the width-of-cut limitation) is cost: about $100. It's an expensive tool to justify unless you're a professional. (Incidentally, a hand slitter can be used to slice strips of wood veneer too.)

Plastic-laminate pieces are typically cut slightly oversize. Then, after they have been glued in place, the overhanging edges are trimmed with a flush-trimming bit in a router. Any router can do the job, but a small router, called a laminate trimmer, is more convenient to use because it's light in weight and can be held in one hand.

Flush-trimming bits come in various diameters and lengths. You don't want anything too big. A ¼-in.-shank trim-

A hand slitter slices strips of this wood-grain vertical-grade laminate off the sheet without making any noise or dust.

mer bit with a ½-in.-long cutting blade can serve double duty by trimming ¼-in. plywood as well as laminate.

After the laminate is glued down and trimmed, the edges will need to be finish filed because a flush-trimming bit really cuts almost flush, but not entirely flush. For this you'll need a fine-cutting laminate file.

LAMINATING THE BOTTOMS AND SIDES OF CABINETS

Since laminate sheets are flimsy unless they're glued to a solid substrate, it is unwise to apply them directly to wall cabinets with recessed bottoms. You first have to glue and brad on a sheet of ¼-in. lauan plywood, exactly as described on pp. 104-105. Then hold the laminate in place, scribe as needed against the back wall, and glue the sheet on.

Contact cement is the glue to use when gluing plastic laminate. You brush, roll, or spray an even layer of the glue on the plastic laminate and the underlayment. When the two glue layers are sufficiently dry, you bring the pieces together and they stick on contact. Contact cement in aerosol form is convenient but more expensive than brush- or roller-applied contact cement. Whichever kind you use, be sure to follow the directions and heed the warnings on the container.

Gluing on a bottom sheet of laminate is a bit tricky, especially if it's a big sheet. The problem is that the sheet is thin and unwieldy, and the contact cement grabs and sticks on contact; you can't stick it on and then shift it around into position. Gluing on big pieces is easier if you have a helper. If you don't, you can lay out several temporary spacers to prevent the sheet

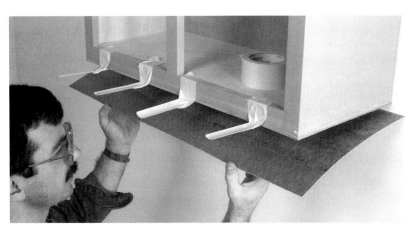

Since sheets of glued laminate stick on contact, it's a good idea to use temporary spacers, such as these mini-blind slats, as a positioning aid. Once the sheet is where you want it, pull the slats out and let the surfaces stick.

from making contact until it's properly positioned. Old Venetian or mini-blind slats make good spacers, and they can be held in place with masking tape on the front of the cabinet (see the bottom photo on the facing page). After the sheet is positioned, pull the spacers out and pat down the laminate. Then, to ensure the strongest possible bond, roll the entire surface with a laminate roller.

Trim the laminate overhangs with a laminate trimmer, as shown in the top photo at right (you can do this immediately after rolling). Then sand the edge with 100-grit paper in a sanding block (see the middle photo at right). Holding the block flat, sand enough to clean off any residual chips and glue and flatten and smooth out any irregularities in the trimmed edge.

The cabinet side panels are glued on after the bottoms. If you will be applying the laminate directly to the side of the old cabinet, make sure the surface is smooth, flat, and free of dust. You can glue directly over painted surfaces if they are sound. If the quality of a surface is questionable, you can glue and brad a layer of ¼-in. lauan plywood to the side and laminate over that. However, if you do this, be aware that it adds to the width of the cabinet more than a thin sheet of laminate, and the plywood should be put on before the bottom piece of laminate. Otherwise, you'll end up seeing the bottom edge of the plywood. Finish-trim laminate overhangs with the laminate trimmer, and sand with 100-grit paper. However, where the laminate side pieces meet the bottom pieces, don't use sandpaper. Instead, finish-file the edges perfectly flush using the laminate file (see the bottom photo at right).

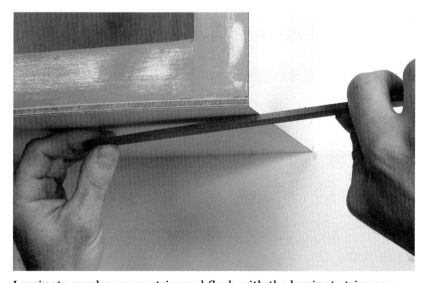

Laminate overhangs are trimmed flush with the laminate trimmer (top). Laminate edges along wood can be smoothed with 100-grit paper in a sanding block (middle). Laminate-to-laminate trimmed edges should be filed smooth with a laminate file (above).

When sheet laminating, glue a whole piece of laminate over the face frames (right), then drill a hole in the sheet to fit the laminate-trimmer bit into and rout out the openings, working clockwise (below right).

LAMINATING THE FACE FRAMES

With the bottoms and sides done, you can turn your attention to the face frames. When you ordered your materials (see pp. 79-80), you chose the method you would use: sheet lamination or strip lamination.

Sheet laminating

With sheet laminating, you fit one large piece of laminate over entire sections of face frame—when one sheet won't do, two or more sheets can be butted together. The face frames and sheets are coated with contact cement, the sheets are positioned (see the top photo on the facing page), stuck down, and smoothed by hand. Then the openings are routed out, and the edges filed or sanded smooth.

Begin the routing by drilling an access hole for the router bit, and then move your laminate trimmer around the opening in a clockwise direction (see the bottom photo on the facing page). Trim the outside edges, and then thoroughly roll the remaining laminate.

Outside corners (where the face-frame piece meets the sides and bottom) are finish-filed square, and inside edges get sanded with a sanding block and 100-grit paper. The inside corners of the cut-out laminate will not be square. They will be rounded because the trimmer bit is round (see the photo above). Although the corners can be filed square, it isn't recommended by laminate manufacturers because a square-cut inside corner can lead to stress cracking. In my own work, I think square inside corners look better, and I have filed away the radius on some laminate jobs—no stress cracking has resulted. I'll let you make your own decision on this.

One way to strip-laminate face frames is to apply oversize pieces and trim off the overhang (top left). The ears that remain where rails meet stiles can be scored with a knife run against a straightedge (top right) and broken off cleanly (above).

Strip laminating

Strip laminating requires much less laminate to do a given job than sheet laminating, but it is a bit more complicated, and therefore more time-consuming. The process is very similar to applying wood veneer, but without the wrapping. You measure, cut, and apply the stile pieces first. You can measure the strips to fit precisely on the width of stiles, or you can cut them slightly oversize, and trim them flush after they're glued on. For our purposes here, I'll focus on the steps for installing laminate pieces oversize. The photos that accompany the discussion show a wood-grain laminate.

Measure the stiles and cut the strips about ½ in. oversize in width and length. Glue them all on, then trim away the excess with the laminate trimmer (see the photo at top left on the facing page). Where rails meet the stiles, small ears will remain, and they are removed almost exactly like wood-veneer ears (see pp. 116-119). As long as you are using vertical-grade laminate, which is quite thin, the material will break very easily if scored using a utility knife. Score lightly at first, then with increased pressure for a few more passes (see the photo at top right on the facing page). Finally, slide the point of the knife under the ear and lift up to break it off cleanly (see the bottom photo on the facing page).

Size and rough-cut rail strips just like the stile strips. Then square-cut one end, hold it in place on the rail, mark the other end, cut it to fit, and glue it on. When you trim the overhanging edges, there will be a radius at the inside corners. With strip lamination, stress cracking is not an issue; the rounded corners can be filed square.

If perchance you goof when applying a strip of laminate, just pull it off (it will break). Soften the contact cement with an acetone-dampened rag, and scrape off the adhesive with a putty knife. Then start all over.

FINISHING TOUCHES

When you're done surfacing a cabinet with laminate, very little touch-up work is required. There are no brad holes to hide, and no stains or lacquer top coats to apply. Still, there are a few things you can do to make the job look better. First, paint all the inside edges a color to match the laminate

The inside edges of laminated face frames should be sanded and then painted.

(see the photo above). Two coats are usually needed. Next, fill all laminate joints with SeamFil (see Resources on pp. 155-157). You can use color putty on laminate, but I prefer to use SeamFil. It comes premixed to many different color matches, or you might have to buy several colors and blend them according to a predetermined "recipe" (SeamFil supplies color recipes for each manufacturer's laminate colors). This filler dries very quickly so you should mix it only in small quantities. Apply with a putty knife to the joint, and wipe off excess filler with an acetone-dampened rag.

On cabinets that have been resurfaced with white or light-colored laminate, 45° and 90° inside corners often show a dark line where the two strips of laminate don't join perfectly. You can eliminate the line with the seam filler. I've also had success applying a very fine bead of appropriately colored silicone caulk. If you squeeze a very small bead on and then wipe it down with a water-dampened finger, it works like a charm.

PUTTING IT ALL TOGETHER

After all the careful planning and cabinet preparation comes the best part of all—putting on the new door and drawer fronts. This is where you'll find yourself standing back quite often to marvel at the work you've done and how incredibly good it all looks. And if you didn't take some pictures of your kitchen before the project began, this is when you're really going to regret it.

DOORS

Whether your doors have traditional hinges or cup hinges, they are attached to the doors before the doors go on the cabinet. Where you place the hinges on the door is mostly a matter of aesthetics.

I usually put traditional hinges about 2 in. from the top and bottom of the doors, because I think that looks best. Consistency of placement is essential: If the hinges are not spaced exactly the same on two doors that meet hinge to hinge, the discrepancy will be obvious. I use a combination square to gauge the distance of all hinges (see the photo at left). To make perfectly centered pilot holes for each screw I use a Vix-Bit. If you don't already have a Vix-Bit, get one (you can order one from almost any tool catalog). You'll wonder how you managed without it.

For concealed cup hinges, I make (or have the door supplier make) the holes for the cups 3½ in. to center from the top and bottom of the doors (see the top photo on the facing page).

Use a combination square to establish consistent spacing for traditional door hinges, then drill pilot holes for the screws with a Vix-Bit.

Hanging doors
with traditional hinges

Hanging traditionally hinged doors is easiest with two people—one person holds the door in position, and the other puts in the screws. But one person can do the job alone if necessary. In either event, you need to mark your door placement along a straight horizontal line that corresponds to the top or bottom of a row of doors. This is done on a length of 2-in.-wide masking tape stretched across the face frame of a run of cabinets. On wall cabinets, put the tape along where the bottom edge of the doors will fall (see the bottom photo at right); on base cabinets, put it along where the top edge of the doors will be.

Stick the tape on loosely, don't leave it there for long, and remove it slowly when you're done with it. Lacquer and masking tape bond to each other exceptionally well, and if you leave the tape on the face frames for more than 15 to 30 minutes, it might not come off as cleanly as you'd like. On one job I was doing, I quickly pulled up a well-adhered strip of masking tape, and the finish on the veneer, all the way to bare wood, came with it. Since then I've been more mindful of the potential for such trouble, and I've followed the cautions above without any further incidents.

Using the reveals that you decided on (see Chapter 3), calculate where the top or bottom line of the cabinet doors should be, and use a chalkline or straightedge to mark its position lightly on the tape. Then measure and mark the side-by-side door positions and reveals along the snapped line.

If you decide to drill your own holes for concealed cup hinges, a homemade jig and a drill press will do the job just fine.

With the door placement and a straight reference line marked out on wide masking tape stuck down to the cabinet fronts, you can hold the door in place and drill the holes for installing traditional hinges.

When hanging the doors, align each one to its marks and install the hinge screw nearest the straight reference line. Use the Vix-Bit to pilot the screw. With that one screw in place, it will be easier for you to hold the door in the proper position. Now realign the door with the bottom line if you need to, and put one screw in the hinge at the opposite end of the door. Don't put the final two screws in the hinges yet, in case there are further adjustments to be made. Work your way along, installing each door in like manner.

When all the adjoining cabinet doors in a run of cabinets are installed, go back and double-check all the side reveals at the tops and bottoms of the doors. It's not unusual to find minor discrepancies, and you can often improve things just by pushing the doors around a bit. This is what I like to call "custom fudging," and it's a part of the work that's to be expected. If you push the door to one side or the other, the mounting plate of the hinge will cock aside slightly. And if you hold the door where you want it and then

put a screw in the cocked plate, you will have tweaked the door into better position. Don't get frustrated if you don't achieve perfectly spaced reveals around each and every door; there are always trade-offs. Stand back and let your eye be the final arbiter when questions of compromise arise.

Custom fudging works only for minor tweaking. If a door is seriously out of position, you may need to remove the hinge screws and reposition the hinge. Fortunately, the hinge plate is big enough that it allows you to move the door a little and still cover the old hole. But the old hole will probably be so close to your new hole that you'll have a tough time trying to get the screw in the new place. So you should plug unwanted screw holes by sharpening a scrap of wood to a point, tapping it into the hole, and breaking or slicing off the excess.

Dealing with warp If, when you close a door, one corner of the latch side meets the frame before the other, something is out of whack—either the cabinet is out of square or the door is warped. A little bit of door warp is usual and acceptable, but it should be "fixed" as best you can. There are two ways to alleviate the problem.

One approach is to loosen the screws in the door wing of one hinge, slide one or more strips of scrap veneer under it, and retighten the screws (see the photo at left). Do this on the hinge that's diagonally opposite the corner of the door that doesn't close all the way, and you'll probably correct the situation. The other method (if you use plastic bumpers on the back side of the door) is simply to shave a bit off

You can adjust the fit of a warped door with traditional hinges by loosening one hinge and sliding scraps of veneer under the plate to shim it out.

the thickness of the door bumper that hits. Do this with a utility knife or a pad sander.

Hanging doors with cup hinges

To hang doors with cup hinges, apply masking tape and mark the door locations as described in the previous section for traditional hinges. Attach the mounting plates to the hinges. Hold the door in an open position, with the plates in place on the stile and the bottom of the door on the straight reference line, and put a screw in each hinge (see the top photo at right). Then close the door to make sure it's on the reference line. Adjust it up or down if necessary (the screws on the plates are in elongated screw holes) and put in the other hinge screws when you're satisfied with the door placement.

Side-to-side adjustment of reveals is accomplished by loosening the screw that holds the cup hinge to the mounting plate (see the bottom photo at right). When your adjustment is complete, firmly tighten the screw. Some refacers complain that the plate-to-hinge screw on Compact 33 hinges tends to come loose over time, but if you use a Pozi screwdriver (instead of a #2 Phillips) and you make sure to tighten the screws securely, loosening shouldn't be a problem.

Dealing with warp Unfortunately, there is no face-frame-mounted cup hinge that has a simple built-in adjustment feature to correct door or cabinet warp—I think some manufacturer should work on the problem. In the meantime, you'll have to try to fix warps by shimming out one hinge, much as described for traditional

Doors with cup hinges are installed with the door in an open position.

Side-to-side adjustments are made by loosening the hinge-to-plate adjustment screw and sliding the arm back and forth. Tighten the screw very securely, preferably with a Pozi screwdriver (shown here).

hinges (see the discussion on the facing page). With cup hinges, though, you'll need to remove the entire cup and add some thin shim material (paper or veneer scraps) to the bottom of the cup hole.

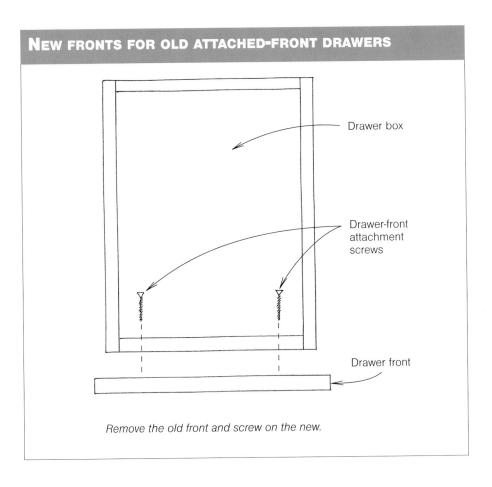

Drawer box

Drawer-front attachment screws

Drawer front

Remove the old front and screw on the new.

DRAWERS AND DRAWER FRONTS

New drawer fronts will be attached to the drawers with screws driven through the front of the drawer box and into the back of the drawer front. But this part of the job is seldom that easy. Your old drawers may have integral fronts, or you may want to replace the old drawer slides with new Euro-style slides. In these instances a little more work is called for before you can install the new drawer fronts.

Installing drawer fronts and slides calls for an assortment of blocks, washers, and screws. If you're a professional refacer, you'll want to keep these items on hand and neatly organized, as I do (see the sidebar on p. 147).

Reusing old drawers

If you are going to reuse the old drawers and their slides, and the old drawers had attached drawer fronts, you simply remove the old fronts, reinstall the drawers, and then install the new drawer fronts (see the drawing above).

On integral-front drawers, the drawer front and the front of the drawer box are one and the same. The sides of the drawer fit into a wide rabbet cut in the back of the drawer front (see the drawing on the facing page). There are two ways to reuse such drawers. One is to cut the overhanging front part off flush with the drawer's top, bottom, and sides. I do this by running the whole drawer through my table saw (with the front facedown on the table),

On an integral-front drawer, one piece of wood serves both as a decorative front and the structural front of the drawer. When refacing, there are two ways to prepare such drawers to receive a new drawer front:

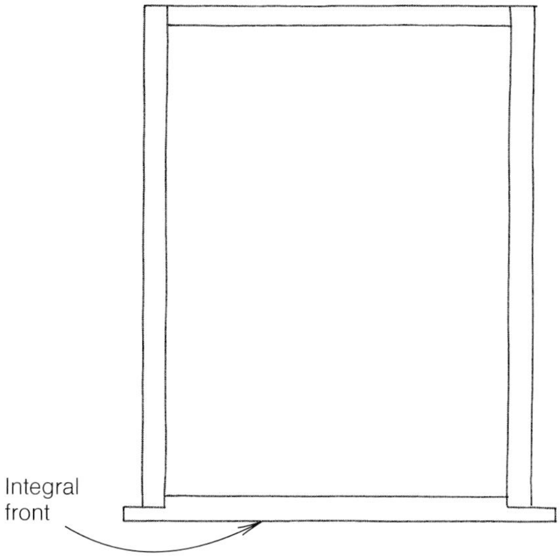

Integral front

Method #1
Cut the overhanging front flush with the top, bottom, and sides of the drawer box.

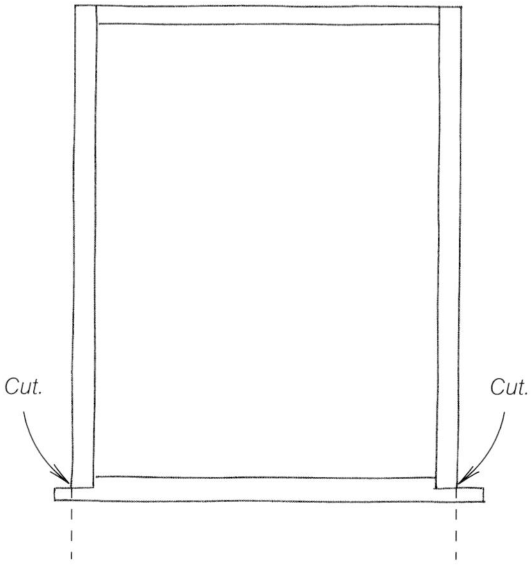

Cut.

Cut.

Method #2
Remove the old front and reinstall a new one between the sides.

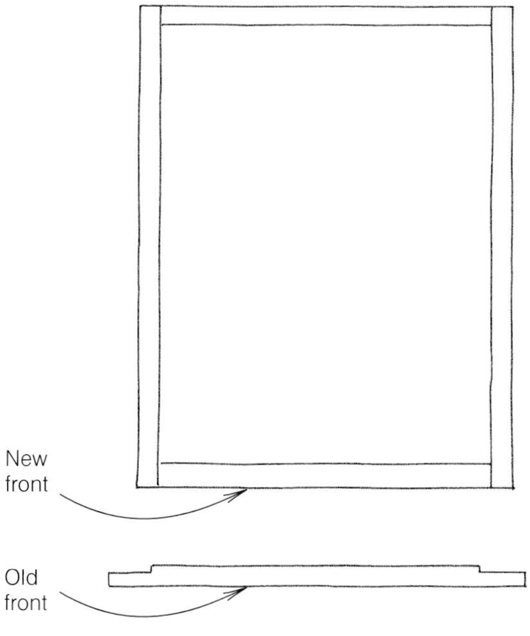

New front

Old front

using the fence as a guide. The result-ing drawer box will need to fit back a little more into the cabinet (by the thickness of the front, which is usually ⅜ in.), and most slides will accommo-date this extra distance. The other way to deal with integral-front drawers is to remove the whole front and fit a new piece of wood between the sides. This is the approach I typically use.

Preparing old drawers for new drawer slides

Euro-style side-mount slides typically take up ½ in. of space on either side of the drawer, so if you intend to upgrade your old drawers with these slides, you will probably have to reduce the width of the old drawers to accommodate the new hardware. Here's my pro-cedure for doing that:

First, measure the drawer opening, subtract 1 in. to get your new drawer width, and compare it to the actual drawer to see how much narrower the drawer needs to be. For example, if the opening is 20½ in. wide, you need a drawer that is 19½ in. wide. If the old drawer is 20¼ in. wide, you know that your drawer needs to be ¾ in. narrower. Figure all of that out and make a note of it before you disassemble the drawer.

If the drawer is assembled with screws, remove them. Nails or staples are more common as drawer fasteners, and usu-ally don't need to be pulled before you knock the box apart. Use a hammer, and perhaps a block of wood, to knock all the joints loose. Even if glued and nailed, old drawer joints usually come apart without much trouble or damage. You can remove finish nails and staples by pulling them all the way through the wood from the back side with a pair of big pliers.

To make a drawer narrower, the front, back, and bottom of the drawer will need to be cut. You can do the cutting on a table saw by setting the fence over to remove the exact amount you calculated before disassembling the box (¾ in. in the previous example). After cutting the pieces to size, reassemble the drawer. You can use glue and brads, or pneumatic staples, or trim screws—or whatever you think will make a good connection.

With Euro-style slides, drawer boxes need to be ¾ in. less in height than the openings to allow enough room for getting the drawer on and off the slides, and out of the cabinet. New drawers can be ordered to the proper size (see pp. 85-86), but old drawers will probably need to be cut down. This can be done on the table saw, either before or after reassembling. If you run an assembled box through the saw, keep any metal fasteners away from the sawblade.

Since there are so many ways that drawers are made, you may have to modify the drawers in some other way that what I have described here. One way or another, old drawers can be trimmed, and you will probably be able to figure out how to deal with an unusual situation. If, upon closer inspection, you'd rather not mess with your old drawers, just make or buy new ones. But you should have decided this long before you get to this stage of the refacing.

Installing new drawer slides

Installing new Euro-style drawer slides in a face-frame cabinet is usually a bit of a challenge. Half of each slide goes on the side of the drawer, and half mounts to the cabinet. Putting the drawer halves on is simply a matter of putting them where they go (refer to the instructions that come with the slide) and screwing them in place. Putting the cabinet halves on is a little more complicated. The front of the slide accepts a screw that fits into the side of the drawer-opening frame (a simple task), but positioning and fastening the back of the slide is where the challenge comes in. The problem is that the back ends must be positioned just so, or the drawer will not close evenly; one side or corner of the soon-to-be-attached drawer front will contact the face frame and a gap will show on the other.

Over the years, I've tried many different methods and made various jigs and other contraptions in an effort to simplify the back placement of these drawer slides. The following approach works for me, and it will work for you. All of this drawer-installation work is much easier to do if the countertop is removed, but it's not a necessity.

Cut an oversize temporary drawer front out of a scrap of ¾-in. plywood (you might use an old cabinet door) and screw it to the front of the drawer. Then, with the slides mounted on the drawer, plastic mounting brackets on the ends of the cabinet slides, and the front of the cabinet slides screwed in place, slide the drawer into the opening and clamp the front to the cabinet

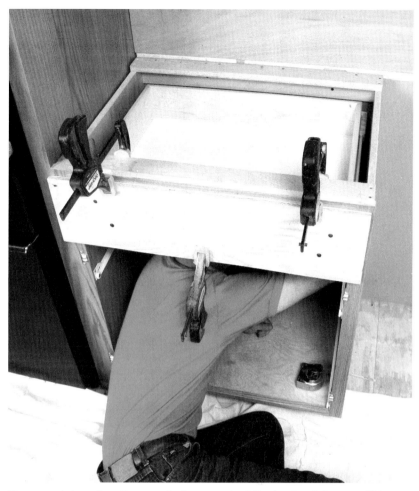

You can determine the exact placement of the back of drawer-slide support brackets by mounting the slides on the drawer and to the front of the cabinet, then screwing on an oversize temporary drawer front, and sliding the drawer into place. Clamp the front to the cabinet, and mark where the brackets are, as shown here. Then remove the drawer, realign the marks, and screw on the bracket.

(see the photo above). This puts the drawer exactly where you want it, and that means the slides are essentially exactly where they should be. From there, it's a relatively simple matter of fastening the back end of the slides. To do this, mark the position of the plastic mounting brackets, remove the drawer, realign the brackets and put in one screw. But before you put the rest of the screws in each bracket (at least

Drawer slides that are attached with mounting brackets can benefit from extra support from a screw into the side of the cabinet. With face-frame cabinets a block will need to be added; washers can be used as shims if needed between the rail and the block.

two will be needed), reinstall the drawer to double-check that it closes evenly. Make minor adjustments if necessary, and then securely fasten the brackets.

With the drawer installed, you can consider that job finished. But for extra security, I often run one more screw through the slide (near the bracket) into the side of the cabinet. The Blum plastic brackets I use are quite sturdy, but I've had experiences where similar brackets have eventually broken, particularly on drawers with heavy loads. So even though it is a bit of a bother, I think the effort is well spent. There are already holes in the slide for the screw.

On face-frame cabinets, the screw goes into a precisely sized block of wood between the cabinet side and slide (see the photo above).

Installing drawer fronts

Like drawer slides, drawer fronts must be installed just so. If a front is crooked or if its side-to-side alignment is off from the front below it, your work is going to look sloppy. Over the years, I've tried various methods for fastening drawer fronts. The best approach I've found entails six steps, which are shown in the photoessay on pp. 148-149. This method generally gives good results. However, if after

#6 X 1-IN. FLAT-HEAD SHEET-METAL SCREWS

Unlike the typical 1-in. wood screw, sheet-metal screws have threads all the way along the length of the shank, and do a better job of securing thin items (like slide rails). For extra holding power, I use these screws instead of the #6 x $^5/_8$-in. screws that come with Euro-style slides.

#8 X 1 $^1/_8$-IN. SUPER-ROUND WASHER-HEAD SCREWS

These coarse-thread wood screws, also known as drawer-front screws, have a large (almost $^1/_2$-in.-dia.) square-drive head. They're ideal for attaching drawer fronts.

#8 X 32 (THREAD) MACHINE SCREWS

These are the screw I use to attach door and drawer pulls. Although screws come with the hardware, they are usually only long enough to be used on door fronts. Longer screws are needed for drawer hardware. I stock various lengths up to 2$^1/_2$ in.

The nuts and bolts of refacing include #10 flat washers, #6 x $^5/_8$-in. wood screws, #6 x 1-in. flat-head sheet-metal screws, super-round washer-head screws, and #8 machine screws with a 32 thread; these are shown left to right in the photo above. Everything packs neatly into a small tote, along with blocks in various sizes (see the photo below right).

The tote contains the essentials I need to install drawer slides, fronts, and hardware. All the screws and washers, with the exception of the washer-head screws, should be readily available at any hardware store. Washer-head screws can be ordered from McFeely's (see Resources on pp. 155-157).

WOOD BLOCKS

I use square wood blocks primarily for solid blocking when I install a screw in the side of drawer slides (see the photo on p. 146). I stock a supply of these blocks, which I cut out of scrap 2x4 lumber. The blocks are all 1$^1/_2$ in. wide by 6 in. long and are ripped to 12thicknesses (from

$^1/_8$ in. to 1$^1/_2$ in., in $^1/_8$-in. increments). As a quick visual key, I label each block with dots (on thin pieces) or with a number. These indicate the thickness of the block, in eighths.

#10 FLAT WASHERS

I use one or more of these washers to shim the metal slide rails out from the blocks if necessary.

#6 X $^5/_8$-IN. WOOD SCREWS

These are the screws typically supplied with drawer slides and cup hinges.

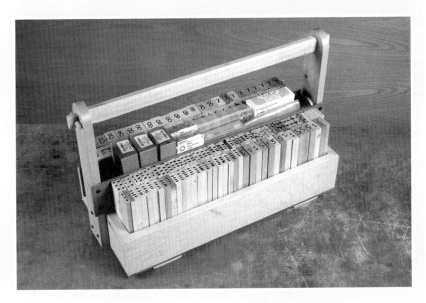

INSTALLING A NEW DRAWER FRONT

1. Use masking tape to measure on and mark out the exact placement of the drawer front.

2. The front will be attached with washer-head screws driven from inside the drawer into the back of the front. Drill a ⅛-in.-dia. hole through the drawer box where you want each screw to go. Most drawers get four screws, one near each corner.

3. Drive in the washer-head screws so that the point projects just a small bit through the front.

4. Close the drawer and make sure it is square in the opening. Carefully align the new front where it will go and hold it there with one hand. Then reach through the nearest door or drawer opening all the way to the back of the drawer, and pull it toward you, so the screw points make small indentations on the back of the drawer front.

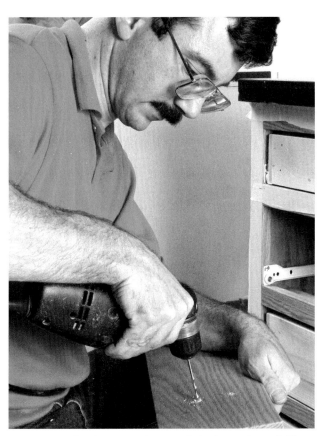

5. Remove the front, and at each indentation, drill a ⅛-in.-dia. pilot hole about ⅜ in. deep. Then drive the washer-head screws through the drawer-box front so they stick out a little farther (¼ in. to ⅜ in).

6. Hold the drawer front against the drawer box so the screw points fit into the pilot holes. Drive in two of the screws. Slide the drawer in and check the fit. It should be dead perfect, and if it is, drive home the other two screws.

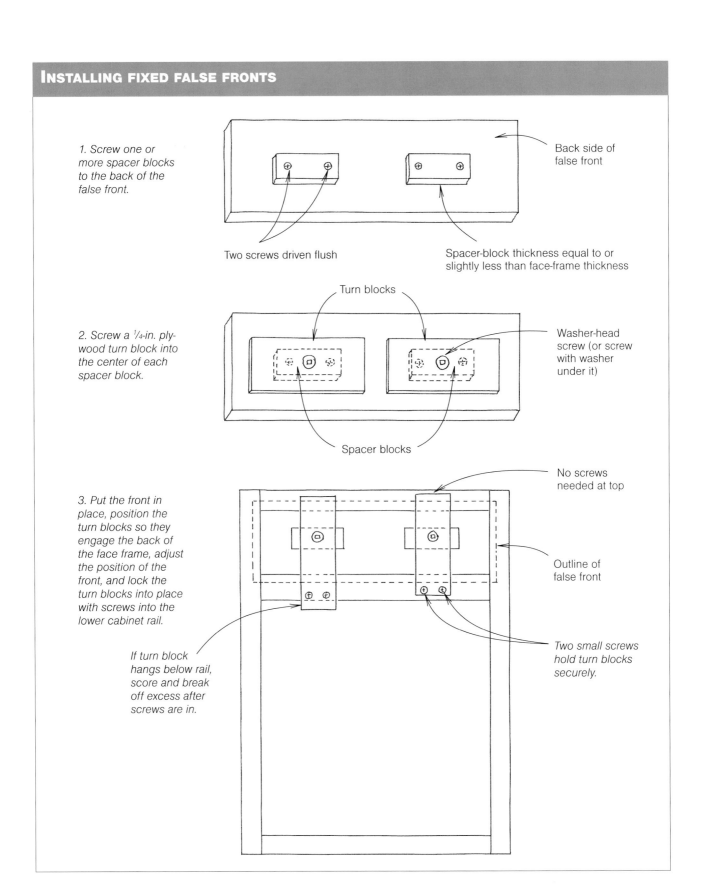

1. Screw one or more spacer blocks to the back of the false front.

Back side of false front

Two screws driven flush

Spacer-block thickness equal to or slightly less than face-frame thickness

Turn blocks

2. Screw a ¼-in. plywood turn block into the center of each spacer block.

Washer-head screw (or screw with washer under it)

Spacer blocks

No screws needed at top

3. Put the front in place, position the turn blocks so they engage the back of the face frame, adjust the position of the front, and lock the turn blocks into place with screws into the lower cabinet rail.

Outline of false front

Two small screws hold turn blocks securely.

If turn block hangs below rail, score and break off excess after screws are in.

driving in two of the screws (Step 6 on p. 149) you find that further adjustment of the front is needed, just back out the two attachment screws and redrill the holes using a ¼-in. bit. The enlarged holes will give you room to jockey the drawer front around into position. Then refasten the front, but this time, instead of driving the screws in firmly, snug them up just enough to hold the front. Install the drawer, close it, and gently knock it into position exactly where it should be. The larger-diameter holes will allow the screw to shift around, and the big washer heads should still cover the holes. When everything is to your satisfaction, you can tighten the two screws and put in the other two.

With the drawers installed, remove the masking tape from the face frame, and stick one bumper on each side.

Installing false drawer fronts on sink base cabinets

False drawer fronts for sink base cabinets can be fixed or movable. Fixed false fronts can be installed very easily, even with the sink and counter in place, using the procedure shown in the drawing on the facing page.

Movable fronts are installed with special drop-front hinges, and tilt trays are installed on the back side of the front. When you install tilt fronts, follow the hinge installation instructions. The hinges are a lot easier to install if you have access to the back side of the cabinet, so if your reface remodeling includes a new sink and/or countertop, install the hinges and trays before you put in the new sink or counter.

PULLS

Pulls—I use the term here to refer to all manner of handles and knobs—are typically attached to doors and drawers with #8 machine screws with a 32 thread. Most hardware that you buy includes such screws, but they are typically only long enough to be used on door fronts that are ¾ in. thick. You'll need longer screws for attaching pulls to new drawer fronts. The exact length you'll need will vary, depending on the thickness of the front and the drawer box, but 2-in.-long screws will generally suffice.

There are no absolute rules for pull placement on door and drawer fronts, so I always ask my customers what they prefer—different folks have different perceptions about what's "correct." I like to put one pull in the center of drawers, even if they're wide, but some people want two pulls on wide drawers. However, do use one centered pull with wide tilt-tray fronts because they will typically be opened only with one hand and the hinges don't function well when the front is pulled from off center. Fixed false fronts do not usually get any pulls.

Using a tape measure, you can measure and mark the placement of each pull's screw hole(s) on masking tape stuck to the front, but you're less liable to make a mistake if you use a homemade or manufactured hardware jig. On one kitchen I did, my helper measured and marked out each hole, then drilled them all, and discovered that the knob on one door was 1 in. lower than all the others. There was no easy way to fix the problem. We could have used a backer plate to hide the blunder, but then all the pulls would have required backer plates, and that would have been as expensive as a new door. Besides, the customer didn't want backer plates. So we ended up buying the new door.

Tool catalogs carry various hardware jigs, but they don't come cheap, and a simple homemade jig will work just as well. The jig I use to mark hole placement on doors is shown in the photo on the facing page. One jig will usually work on all the doors in a kitchen (and for that matter, on different kitchens). But for drawer fronts, I've found a jig is not so universally handy, so I still measure and mark out each screw hole individually. Needless to say, I work very carefully.

If you'll be using #8 screws, drill the holes with a 3/16-in.-dia. bit. If you hold a scrap block of wood behind where you're drilling, the bit won't splinter the wood as it comes through.

VALANCES

One of the hallmarks of a well-crafted kitchen (reface or otherwise) is a valance that fits tightly between the face frames it adjoins. Installing a valance is something like installing veneer on the face-frame rails: It has to fit tight at both ends or it will look sloppy. If I ever stop by your house, this is something I'm sure to look at. Here's how to do the work to high standards:

Begin by measuring the width of the valance space, and square-cut the valance 1/4 in. to 3/8 in. longer. A power miter box is the best tool to use for this. If you have anything besides a straight valance, make the cuts so the design is centered. Measure carefully—

there is no way to stretch or otherwise salvage a valance that has been cut too short.

Hold the valance up in place, with the last end you cut butted against the cabinet exactly where it will go (the other end will overlap the cabinet face a bit). If the cut on the butted side isn't exact (you'll see a gap of light at the top or bottom), adjust the saw and recut as needed to get a perfect fit on this one cut. Exercise great caution— don't take off any more wood off than you have to. Then go through this same process on the other end.

At this point, the valance, still a tad too long, should have the precise cut needed on both ends, and you should still have the exact cut for the last side you fit set on your saw. Now double-check the length of the opening, and cut the valance 1/16 in. longer, using that saw setting on the appropriate end. Put the valance in place, and push on one or both of the side cabinets to open the space enough for the valance. If it's too tight, cut a tad more. Once the valance is in place, drive a couple of screws through the adjoining cabinet stiles into the ends of the valance. Make the holes carefully (use a pilot hole and a clearance hole).

MOLDINGS

I cut all my moldings to size with a power miter box and fasten them on with a pneumatic finish nailer. If you hand-nail moldings, it's a good idea to predrill a small hole for each finish nail you use, especially when working with hardwoods. Also use carpenter's wood glue on outside mitered pieces.

Simple homemade hardware jigs like this one can ensure consistent and proper placement of holes for screws used to fasten door and drawer pulls.

For installing long lengths of molding, like the soffit-to-cabinet molding, you want the piece to be straight and spaced the same distance above the top of all the doors. I get the best job here by hauling out the masking tape once again and sticking it down where the molding will go. Then I measure and mark the bottom edge and snap a line on the tape. The strip of molding is nailed on over the tape. Afterwards, I lightly slice along the bottom of the molding with a utility knife and pull the tape free. The tape is so thin that the half that remains under the molding does not show.

That's it—the job is done. We've gone through the process of kitchen cabinet refacing from beginning to end. Now it's time for you to take on your own kitchen or other people's kitchens— whatever the case may be. I wish you the very best in your endeavors.

RESOURCES

Now that you've read this book, I hope you've come to realize just how simple it is to do kitchen cabinet refacing. You don't have to be an accomplished cabinetmaker or a professional in the building trades to make your old kitchen new and beautiful again. And you don't need a fully equipped workshop, either. But you do need some good sources for materials and tools, and many of these items may not be available in your local community. With that thought in mind, I offer this compendium of suppliers for refacing materials, miscellaneous supplies, hardware, and tools. You should be able to find anything and everything you need through one or more of these sources.

A listing of this nature can never be comprehensive. If you know of or discover other sources for refacing-related supplies that are not listed here, please let me know so that I can include them in future editions.

REFACING MATERIALS

So many companies make doors in this country that their names would probably fill a book. Here are just a few door manufacturers who do business with refacers. For the most part, the companies listed here also offer veneer, plywood, valances, moldings, and drawers as well as finished doors.

Companies whose names are preceded by an asterisk (*) deal with professionals only. The other companies cater primarily to pros but will also work with savvy homeowners (that's you if you've read this book). I have no first-hand experience with any of these companies except Concepts in Wood, although I have every reason to believe they're all reputable suppliers. The Yellow Pages of your local telephone directory and advertisements in woodworking magazines are other places you can look for suppliers.

*Cabinet Factory
PO Box 1748
LaCrosse, WI 54602-1748
(800) 237-1326
FAX (608) 781-3667
www.cabinetfactory.com

Concepts in Wood
4021 New Court Ave.
Syracuse, NY 13206
(315) 463-8084
FAX (315) 463-1157

*Conestoga Wood Specialties
245 Reading Rd.
East Earl, PA 17519-0158
(800) 964-3667
FAX (717) 445-3409

*Horizon CNC Products
3275 Brushy Creek Rd.
Greer, SC 29650
(864) 877-8608
FAX (864) 848-1334
(rigid-thermal-foil doors and moldings only)

*Keystone Wood Specialties
PO Box 10127
2225 Old Philadelphia Pike
Lancaster, PA 17605-0127
(800) 233-0289
(717) 299-6288
FAX (800) 253-0805

Martin Cabinetware
1060 Colborne St.
London, ON
CANADA N6A 4B2
(519) 679-1297
FAX (519) 679-2410
www.mirror.org/cabinetware

*Meridian Products
124 Earland Dr., Building #2
New Holland, PA 17557-1503
(717) 355-7700
FAX (717) 355-2517

National Wood Products
PO Box 1479
1041 Hal Greer Blvd.
Huntington, WV 25716-1479
(800) 624-3511
(304) 529-0499
FAX (304) 529-0469

Northeast Cabinet Door
33 Morrell St.
West Roxbury, MA 02132
(617) 469-5445
FAX (617) 469-0770

Quality Doors
621 Hall St.
Cedar Hill, TX 75104
(800) 950-3667
(214) 291-2420
FAX (214) 291-9770
(This company sells its doors nationwide through dealers and home centers. Call for the name of a distributor near you.)

MISCELLANEOUS REFACING SUPPLIES

The companies listed here offer individual refacing components; all will deal with the homeowner/craftsman.

CCF Industries
1300 Hulton Rd.
Verona, PA 15147
(800) 581-3683
(412) 793-7959
FAX (412) 793-8234
(dovetailed drawers in various materials, including ½-in. Baltic-birch plywood)

Eagle Woodworking
1130 East St.
Tewksbury, MA 01876
(800) 628-4849
FAX (508) 640-1501
(solid-maple dovetailed drawers)

Kampel Enterprises
8930 Carlisle Rd.
Wellsville, PA 17365
(717) 432-9688
FAX (717) 432-5601
(manufacturer of SeamFil)

Klingspor's
PO Box 3737
Hickory, NC 28603-3737
(800) 228-0000
(800) 872-2005
(mail-order catalog of sanding and finishing supplies)

Oakwood Veneer Company
3642 W. Eleven Mile Rd.
Berkley, MI 48072
(800) 426-6018
(810) 542-9979
(veneers of all types and species)

Scherr's Cabinet & Doors
5315 Burdick Expressway East
Rt. #5, Box #12
Minot, ND 58701
(701) 839-3384
FAX (701) 852-6090
(ready-to-assemble cabinets and unfinished doors of various kinds)

HARDWARE

The companies listed here offer hinges, slides, lazy Susans, pulls, handles, and knobs. Most will send product information or a catalog on request. Contact manufacturers for the name of a distributor near you.

Amerock Corporation
PO Box 7018
Rockford, IL 61125-7018
(815) 969-9655
FAX (815) 969-6138
(manufacturer of drawer slides, lazy Susans, and opening hardware)

Blue Heron Enterprises
842 East Douglas Ave.
Bellingham, WA 98226
(800) 360-647-2024
(360) 647-2024
(manufacturer of the slide-out mechanism shown on p. 40)

Julius Blum
Highway 16—Lowesville
Stanley, NC 28164
(800) 438-6788
(manufacturer of European hardware, including side-mount drawer slides and Compact 33 series cup hinges)

McFeely's
1620 Wythe Rd.
PO Box 11169
Lynchburg, VA 24506-1169
(800) 443-7937
FAX (800) 847-7136
(mail-order source for fasteners and
finishing supplies)

Rev-A-Shelf
2409 Plantside Dr.
Jeffersontown, KY 40299
(800) 626-1126
FAX (502) 491-2215
(manufacturer of lazy Susans and kitchen
organizational accessories)

Woodworker's Hardware
PO Box 180
Sauk Rapids, MN 56379
(800) 383-0130
FAX (800) 207-0180
(mail-order catalog of hardware of all
kinds, including a good selection of solid-
brass pulls)

The Woodworkers' Store
4365 Willow Dr.
Medina, MN 55340
(800) 279-4441
FAX (612) 478-8395
(mail-order source of miscellaneous hardware and some woodworking tools)

TOOLS

Most of the tools you'll need for refacing
are common woodworking tools that are
sold locally at hardware stores and home
centers. Some of the companies listed
here offer the specialty tools mentioned
in this book; others have catalogs that
feature a vast selection of tools, as well
as some hardware supplies that you are
unlikely to find at local retail outlets.

Constantine's
2050 Eastchester Rd.
Bronx, NY 10461
(800) 223-8087
FAX (800) 253-WOOD

JCM Industries
774 State Road 13, #9
Jacksonville, FL 32259
(800) 669-5519
(mail-order source for tools for working
with plastic laminate)

Klenk Industries
20 Germay St.
Wilmington DE 19804
(800) 327-5619
(manufacturer of laminate snips)

Lee Valley Tools
PO Box 1780
Ogdensburg, NY 13669-0490
(800) 871-8158

Professional Kitchen Craftsman
PO Box 1117
Moravia, NY 13118
(315) 497-9618
(Veneer Slick, Refacer's MUT)

Tradesman Publishing `27.95`

`15.95 total`

Simp'l Products
264 Fordham Place
Box 187
City Island, NY 10464
(718) 885-3314
(manufacturer of Laminatrol cutting
guide)

Woodcraft
210 Wood County Industrial Park
PO Box 1686
Parkersburg, WV 26102-1686
(800) 225-1153
FAX (304) 428-8271

Woodworker's Supply
1108 N. Glen Rd.
Casper, WY 82601
(800) 645-9292

FURTHER READING

As far as I know, this is the first and only book ever written about cabinet refacing. There are a few videos on the market that address the subject, but I wouldn't recommend any that I've seen. In-depth magazine articles are rare. However, *Fine Homebuilding* magazine ran a good piece in issue #81 (April/May 1993). Rex Alexander, the author of that article, presents a different refacing technique (using unfinished iron-on veneer), which just goes to illustrate the variety of refacing opinions and methods of work.

For an up-to-date, in-depth discussion of refacing and more conventional kitchen remodeling, you might want to subscribe to *Professional Kitchen Craftsman,* an eight-page newsletter. The focus of this newsletter is not exclusively on refacing, but the craft is a major subject. Write *Professional Kitchen Craftsman,* PO Box 1117, Moravia, NY 13118; (315) 497-9618. A one-year subscription (six issues) costs $15.

Two books that you may find useful are Jim Tolpin's *Building Traditional Kitchen Cabinets* and my own book, *Making Plastic-Laminate Countertops.* Tolpin's book is a well-rounded how-to text that covers everything from kitchen design to building and installing cabinets. It has chapters on making doors and drawers and finishing your work—this is information that could prove useful to a cabinet refacer. The countertop book will be a great help if you intend to reface with plastic laminate. If you are planning to do your own finishing, you may want

to consult *Spray Finishing* by Andy Charron and *The Woodfinishing Book* by Michael Dresdner. All four of these books are available from The Taunton Press (63 South Main St., Newtown, CT 06470).

There are literally hundreds of books and magazines on kitchen planning and design. Rather than steer you toward particular publications, I would suggest instead that you spend some time browsing in a well-stocked library or bookstore. The pictures and information you find will be extremely helpful in the planning stages. It should give you plenty of fodder for ideas on kitchen layout, cabinetry, finishes, and appliances.

No discussion of information sources would be complete without mentioning the Internet. If you're familiar with the "net," then you already know how useful it can be as a research tool. If you have not yet experienced the Internet, you're in for a pleasant surprise.

With a personal computer, a modem to connect your computer to the phone line, and an Internet access provider, you can search millions of sites worldwide for information on virtually any subject. Through your computer, you can reach product manufacturers and various technical representatives. You can compare products and prices, and even order materials. You can also swap stories with other amateur and professional craftsmen and request how-to help by posting questions on electronic bulletin boards

that are devoted to specific subjects. You can also participate in chat groups and actually "talk" to other people on-line.

As vast as the Internet is, I haven't yet found much directly related to cabinet refacing, except for the web pages of some product suppliers. But that may well change because the Web is constantly growing and evolving. If you do venture onto this exciting information highway, here are four places to start: Woodweb (www.woodweb.com), The Oak Factory (www.theoak.com), Knots (www.taunton.com/fwdisc), and Breaktime (www.taunton.com/fhdisc). Each has bulletin-board discussion groups where you can learn a lot. Better yet, each of these locations has a good list of "links" that will take you to other web sites with related information.

If you have a question about refacing or about something you've read in this book, feel free to post it on the Breaktime bulletin board. I surf through there regularly and will do my best to help you out.

If the very thought of computer research makes your stomach churn with anxiety, let me put your fears to rest. The entire thing is very easy to use. You needn't have a degree in computer science or even a computer. Many public libraries have Internet access and periodically offer courses on using the Internet. If you want to know more, I suggest you inquire at your local library about an introductory class. That's how I got started.

GLOSSARY

Base shoe Small molding installed against the floor at the bottom of baseboard molding.

Blind corner Hard-to-access storage space inside a corner base cabinet.

Bumper pad A small protective piece of felt, rubber, cork, or plastic applied (usually in pairs) to the back of door and drawer fronts to muffle sound and soften the shock of closing the door or drawer.

Butt joint A simple joint composed of two flat surfaces that meet each other. Butt joints are generally glued and reinforced with nails or screws.

Composite material Manmade sheets of "wood" assembled from wood chips or fibers that are bonded together with synthetic resins. *See also* Medium-density fiberboard. Particleboard.

Countersink To remove wood around the end of a hole so the head of a screw can be driven flush with the surface.

Cove molding Molding with a concave face.

Close-grained Describes wood with small pores and inconspicuous grain. Maple and cherry are close-grained woods.

Ear A small section of veneer that overlaps adjoining rails or stiles after a face-frame member is wrapped. Veneer ears must be removed.

Extension strip A strip of wood that may be added to the inside of cabinet rails and stiles before veneering to accommodate the layout of new doors and drawer fronts.

Face frame A wood framework attached to the front of a cabinet. The frame gives the cabinet stability and provides a wide face for mounting the doors.

False front A drawer front without a drawer, typically found on sink base cabinets.

Filler strips A piece of wood installed between cabinet face frames when the cabinets are installed. They are used to extend the front of a cabinet so it will fit a given space or to provide extra room at a corner for opening adjoining drawers.

Flexible veneer Wood veneer that is bonded to a paper backing.

Flush Describes surfaces that are exactly even with each other (in the same plane).

Frame-and-panel Doors and drawer fronts that consist of a central panel surrounded by a perimeter framework. *See also* Plank. Slab.

Frameless cabinet A cabinet without a face frame, whose doors close against the ends of the cabinet sides.

Medium-density fiberboard (MDF) A fine-grained composite material made from wood fibers.

Mullions Thin pieces of wood used to create divisions between glass in a door.

Open-grained Describes wood with large pores and distinctive grain. Oak is an open-grained wood.

Overlay The amount of door or drawer front that overlaps a cabinet front. Hinges are available in various overlay versions.

Plank A non-frame-and panel door or drawer-front style made using solid wood.

Plastic laminate A durable surfacing material composed primarily of layers of kraft paper impregnated with phenolic resins and pressed into a solid sheet. Formica is one common brand name.

PSA Pressure-sensitive adhesive, the glue that comes pre-applied to peel-and-stick flexible veneers.

Particleboard A composite material made from wood chips, flakes, and shavings.

Peninsula A section of cabinetry that juts out into a room and is accessible from two sides and one end.

Rail A horizontal or cross member of a door or cabinet frame.

Refacing The craft of covering the exterior of old cabinets with new material and installing new doors and drawer fronts.

Reveal The space between adjoining doors and drawer fronts.

Rigid thermal foil (RTF) Describes doors made by heat-forming a single sheet of PVC plastic (vinyl) over the face of a door blank of medium-density fiberboard. The vinyl is the foil.

Slab A flat door consisting of a plastic or wood layer applied over a core of composite material.

Soffit The area between the ceiling and the top of the wall cabinets, when it is boxed in.

Stile A vertical or upright frame member of a door or cabinet frame.

Toe kick The recessed section at the bottom of base cabinets. The toe kick allows people to stand close to the cabinets without bumping their toes.

Valance A decorative board installed between wall cabinets on either side of a window. The valance is often used to hide light fixtures.

Veneer A thinly sliced sheet of wood.

INDEX

BOOK PUBLISHER: Jim Childs

ACQUISITIONS EDITOR: Julie Trelstad

EDITORIAL ASSISTANT: Karen Liljedahl

EDITOR: Ruth Dobsevage

DESIGNER: Henry Roth

LAYOUT ARTIST: Susan Fazekas

PHOTOGRAPHER, EXCEPT WHERE NOTED: Susan Kahn

ILLUSTRATOR: Herrick Kimball

TYPEFACE: Frutiger Light

PAPER: 70-lb. Moistrite Matte

PRINTER: Quebecor Printing/Hawkins, Church Hill, Tennessee